Look up – Your redemption draws nigh

Contents

introduction

Matthew 24:3 *Now as he sat on the Mount of Olives, the disciples came to him privately saying, "tell us, when will these things be? And what will be the sign of your coming, and of the end of the age?*

The popularity of end time discussions has grown in recent years, especially with escalating apocalyptic events during the 21st century. What do the words *end times* mean? With human understanding, end times is a duration of time before the end of all things. Predominantly, the church understands the end times as the time from when Jesus ascended to heaven until he returns in glory. The end times also refers to Satan's temporary rule to Christs eternal reign; time is the transition period. During this age, the devil is the *God of this world* (2 Corinthians 4:4) all though he was defeated through the cross and resurrection he still holds influential power until the eternal rule of Christ.

The spiritual end time battle rages between two Kingdoms and humans are caught up in the midst of it. The victory was sealed through the blood of Jesus Christ, nevertheless, the world is marching towards a new world (or new normal as some would say), a time when people must choose who they belong to, Satan or Jesus? There will be no middle ground once the *mark of the beast* is enforced. This final era has been cut short by God to a 7-year period known as the tribulation. There are two main reasons for God cutting short this time. First, the number seven is the biblical number of perfection and completion. God created the world in 6 days and rested on the 7th, the initiation of the 7-day week was enforced. The end times are therefore completed within those final 7 years and will put an end to sin and Israel's unbelief. Daniel 9:24 **"Seventy weeks are determined upon thy people and upon thy holy city**, to finish the transgression, and to make an end of sins, and to make reconciliation for iniquity, and to bring in everlasting righteousness, and to seal up the vision and prophecy, and to anoint the most Holy". Secondly, this time must be cut short for the sake of the elect (Matthew 24:22) as no flesh would survive without Gods intervention. Some flesh must be saved ready for the population explosion during the 1,000-year reign of Christ when everlasting righteousness is ushered in through Christ. (Isaiah 65:20).

The end times discussed will be ensued after the significant date of May the 14th 1948; the year Israel was declared a nation. Jesus spoke of the signs during the final generation saying, *truly I tell you, this generation will certainly not pass away until all these things have happened* (Matthew 24:34). Some have miss-understood the meaning of *this generation* as being those Jesus was speaking too at that time, but he was talking about the final generation who will see all these signs. There is no doubt that all the things discussed in Matthew 24:3-30 (Persecution, famines, earthquakes, wars, false prophets, betrayal, and wickedness) have occurred these last 2 millennial, but never have they occurred with such frequency and intensity. There is a great convergence happening in our midst, the signs are escalating and intensifying. The devil is using movements in the name of "global warming" or "climate change" to obscure the end time signs. Through deception and blatant lies he has managed to conceal the prophecy of Jesus to the unsuspecting masses.

Israel is the only nation to be born in a day (Isaiah 66:8) and is considered Gods focal point, the apple of his eye (Deuteronomy 32:10). The birth of Israel initiated the generational end time clock before the return of Jesus Christ. A generation according to Psalm 90:10 - *our days may come to seventy years, eighty, if our strength endures.* This puts the biblical span of a generation between 70-80 years. Mathematically speaking 70 years finished in May 2019, we have now entered the years of endurance. 2019 began with the seemingly apocalyptic Covid pandemic, the time when global events accelerated, and the beast system began to show its ugly face via certificates of vaccination and the militarising of the police with enforced controlling technology.

The enemy knows his time is short, the push for a global government through Agenda 2030 and the *great reset* initiative have entered the world stage, no longer concealed in the shadows of illuminati secrets or the hidden arm of freemasonry. Christians alive today live in the time the prophets of old dreamed of because our redemption draws near! Yet many are spiritually asleep believing this time is no different to any other time in history. The truth is, this time is very different and unless there is a great awakening soon, we will be swept along with the ways of the new world order.

The following highlighted signs mentioned below are taken from the words of Jesus Christ in Matthew 24:3-30.

Matthew 24:4-30 *Jesus answered: "Watch out that no one* **deceives** *you. For many will come in my name, claiming, 'I am the Messiah,' and will deceive many. You will hear of* **wars and rumors of wars** *but see to it that you are not alarmed. Such things must happen, but the end is still to come. Nation will rise against nation, and* **kingdom against kingdom***. There will be* **famines** *and* **earthquakes** *in various places. All these are the beginning of birth pains. "Then you will be handed over to be* **persecuted** *and put to death, and you will be hated by all nations because of me. At that time many will turn away from the faith and will betray and hate each other, and many false prophets will appear and deceive many people. Because of the* **increase of wickedness***, the love of most will grow cold, but the one who stands firm to the end will be saved. And this gospel of the kingdom will be* **preached in the whole world** *as a testimony to all nations, and then the end will* come. "So, when you see standing in the holy place 'the abomination that causes desolation, 'spoken of through the prophet Daniel—let the reader understand— then let those who are in Judea flee to the mountains. Let no one on the housetop go down to take anything out of the house. Let no one in the field go back to get their cloak. How dreadful it will be in those days for pregnant women and nursing mothers! Pray that your flight will not take place in winter or on the Sabbath. For then there will be great distress, unequalled from the beginning of the world until now—and never to be equaled again. "If those days had not been cut short, no one would survive, but for the sake of the elect those days will be shortened. At that time if anyone says to you, 'Look, here is the Messiah!' or, 'There he is!' do not believe it. For false messiahs and false prophets will appear and perform great signs and wonders to deceive, if possible, even the elect. See, I have told you ahead of time. "So, if anyone tells you, 'There he is, out in the wilderness,' do not go out; or, 'Here he is, in the inner rooms,' do not believe it. For as lightning that comes from the east is visible even in the west, so will be the coming of the Son of Man. Wherever there is a carcass, there the vultures will gather. "Immediately after the distress of those days "'the sun will be darkened, and the moon will not give its light; the stars will fall from the sky, and the heavenly bodies will be shaken.' "Then will appear the **sign of the Son of Man** in heaven. And then all the peoples of the earth will mourn when they see the Son of Man coming on the clouds of heaven, with power and great glory.

Deception – the ways the enemy deceives

Deceived by false prophets

From the dawn of humanity that serpent of old known as the devil has always operated through deception. One of Satan's master tricks is convincing the world that he does not exist. Hiding behind false Gods and appearing as an angel of light, the devil can lead many down the path of destruction without them knowing it.

The onslaught of the enemy against the church has been relentless, but today the devil has switched up his tactics, at least in the Western church... for now. In the past Satan would physically attack and kill the body of Christ, this still happens in many places. However, the more cunning approach, is to attack the church from within. The old approach was to kill physically and the new one is to kill spiritually.

The devil does it primarily through the wolves in sheep's clothing, the many anti-Christs who have slithered into the pull pits; *they have a form of Godliness but deny its power (2 Timothy 3:5).* They stand in the pulpits and preach a twisted self-orientated version of the gospel, *the best life now* version. They may say something such as, *when you understand grace, you know that you can continue in sin and be forgiven.* There is an element of truth   to this, but grace does not provide a license to sin (Romans 6:15), instead it should lead us away from it. Those who truly repent are indeed forgiven (John 1:9) but repentance means we turn from that which we know is wrong. The enemy continues to ask, *did God really say?* The word of God should therefore be the anchor to our souls and a light to our paths, so we can understand what God really said.

Satan desires to provide a counterfeit version of the true Christ by taking something from God and manipulating it for his own purposes. In Matthew 4 the devil used the word of God and attempted to trap Jesus;

Jesus used the word of God to defend its miss-application. The trap of the enemy is avoided when we are well schooled with the word of God. Sometimes verses are taken out of context such as John 3:16 that states Gods great love for the world by sending Jesus to save humanity. Some may say that *God is too loving to send someone to hell* based upon verses such as this. This proves the verse is taken out of context because in John 3:18 the bible says, *there is no judgement for one who believes in him. But anyone who does not believe in him has already been judged for not believing in Gods one and only son.* If God would not send anyone to hell, then his righteousness is discarded because a perfect record is required to enter heaven, a record only the blood of Jesus has wiped clean. The whole scope of God's word is required to be prepared to deal with the enemy's deception.

Deceived by Distraction

The enemy degrades the power of the Christian by the invitation of distraction. If he can keep Christians busy with worldly affairs, social media, the news, the latest TV show, relationships, or work commitments, then he can stunt the growth of a believer. If a believer is presented with a carefree lifestyle which prevents them deepening their relationship with God, then deceiving them is easier labor for the devil. This is one way so much false teaching has been able to spread like wildfire within the church. Having an easy life does not necessarily mean we are living in God's blessing, if that was so then Jesus and the disciples were not blessed! The devil knows that making life easy does not build character and does not prepare someone for the trials that will inevitably come. Therefore, those who believe God is good only when things are good usually fall away when trials arrive. Learning to focus more on God should be a believer's earthly mission, the more He is magnified the smaller our problems become.

The tribulation deception

During the tribulation there will be a time when the *mark of the beast* will be enforced. A time when every person on earth will have a choice to take the mark and pledge allegiance to the enemy or refuse and be killed. Revelation 13:16 "And he causes all, both small and great, rich and poor, free and bond, to receive a mark in their right hand, or in their foreheads:" The deception will be so vast and great that it would seem impossible not to fall into the devil's trap. The mark will be heralded as a good thing and something that will be convenient and make life easier. Convenience is always a tool used by the enemy to lure people into a life without God. The beast will appear to have all power and authority (Revelation 13:5) and deceive the world through signs and wonders (Revelation 13:13). Should the church be here during this time, now is a perfect time to be filled with the word of God so we will not be deceived. This so-called *convenience* would be something like this; a technological implant or barcode that can be scanned and accessed into a computer data base. This mark could be like a QR code, a simple numeric code that enables access to finances, medical records, and documentation, very convenient indeed.

Throughout the church age the wheat and the tares have grown up together, the great harvest is still to come at the end of age. The wheat and tares will become more distinct during the tribulation as people are forced to be for the enemy or against. True believers in Christ will not be deceived into taking the mark for they are sealed by the Holy Spirit (2 Corinthians 1:22, Ephesians 4:30). The middle ground is removed, no more standing on the fence and being indecisive, a commitment must be made. The arrival of the anti-Christ will be according to the works of Satan (2 Thessalonians 2:9) which means he will arrive through lies and deception. The greatest deception during the tribulation is making the world believe that this is all for the good of humanity, it must take place to *save the planet* from climate change and extinction.

Christians around the world suffer profusely for their faith, many are ostracized and marginalized by society. As cruel and sadistic as this is, Satan is advancing and ushering in his final rebellion before the return of Jesus Christ. Animosity will be stirred up against Christians and Jews to such a degree that many will agree for them to be killed. Revelation 6:4 Then another horse came out, a fiery red one. Its rider was given power to take peace from the earth and to make people kill each other. To him was given a large sword. All Satan would need to do is control a narrative that puts a negative spotlight on believers. How could he do that? Perhaps the devil would say that believers in Christ are standing in the way of *saving the planet.* Perhaps believers will lay hands on the sick for them to be healed instead of staying 6 feet away (the same depth that people are buried). Perhaps Christians will expose the lies and pronounce the soon coming judgement for those who do not repent along with the eternal hope found in Christ. Whatever the reason, the hatred will be stirred up by demonic forces, the same Spirits that caused the Jews to shout *crucify him, crucify him! (John 19:6).* The Christian response should be love and prayer, for this overcomes evil, *repay evil for good (Matthew 5:38-48).* All the forces of evil will be marching during the tribulation, but even then, God is still in control, and he can surely see His people through it!

Deception through mainstream media, music, and propaganda

9

Mainstream media... The mainstream media controls the narrative. During recent years the mainstream media seems to have been hijacked by the devil. It is no longer about journalists seeking to find the truth, it is about a global narrative conditioning people for the soon coming *new world order*. Anyone can be painted as a villain or a hero depending on what side of the story is being told. The world saw Trump as a villain because of how he was portrayed on the mainstream stage. Some called him a racist because of his radical stance on things like *illegal* immigration (1); some thought he was a liar and was doing deals with Ukraine behind the backs of the American people (2). Palestinians hated him because of moving the American embassy to Jerusalem (3). Whatever he did was always blown up to hyper proportions by the media. They did the same with Covid when displaying empty shelves due to people panicking (4). They have done the same with Zelensky by showing him as a hero by refusing to leave Ukraine when the Russians invaded (5). The mainstream controls any narrative they want...especially spreading fear and animosity or unity according to how they want it. The news does not show the full story, they only show what they want you to see. That is not how the news once was, but unfortunately it has become this. Was Trump a villain? Zelensky a hero? Covid a pandemic? Critical thinkers will look deeper and find out the truth. Learning not to depend on mainstream news is imperative to discover the truth.

Music... Corruption in the music industry has been revealed over the years. Artist's renown for "selling their soul to the devil" has always been a topic for discussion. It is no surprise that the devil would use music to convey a message, after all, he was a cherub in heaven who guarded Gods throne and would have worshipped just like all other angels (Ezekiel 28:14). The devil knows the power and influence of music better than humans. Over the years, the music industry has thrown out mottos such like;

welcome to the good life, good girl gone bad, follow your heart or *trust your feelings,* or the more famous expression *I did it my way.* The devil has promoted music to create a following of self-centered people, the opposite of the selfless life God invites us to pursue. The much darker agenda in the music industry is the subliminal messages being told. Here are a couple examples in recent years.

Taylor Swift created a song called *you need to calm down.* This song was created to advocate the LGBT community and was aimed at silencing the *haters* or those considered as homophobic. The music video to this song shows a group of *haters* with scruffy hair and some teeth missing with signs saying *homosexuality is a sin.* All though it is not clear this group of *haters* refers to Christians, who else would potentially use this sign?

Another song worth mentioning was sung by Madonna at the 2019 Eurovision. The following is a sample of the lyrics of a song called *the future…*

Not everyone is coming to the future.

Not everyone here is learning from the past.

Not everyone can come to the future.

Not everyone here is gona last (gona last).

The performance was extremely sinister. Madonna was wearing a black cape and outfit and had a patch over her eye. Some performers had gas masks and fell to the ground when touched by Madonna – at one point the performers are lying as if dead while Madonna sings the chorus! The crowd went wild after the performance, little did they know the song was about them!. That same year the pandemic began in China before spreading to the rest of the world. Those lyrics are demonic and evil, but many do not recognise the enemy in the song. Some would say *it's just entertainment.* This is exactly what the enemy would want people to think.

    Propaganda… Until recent years propaganda was something seen mostly in Communist nations such as

China, North Korea, and Russia. However, we are seeing a shift from democracy to a more government-controlled state. The grand shift began taking shape once Covid arrived. All citizens had to adhere to the new rules and regulations being imposed by governments. Countries like Australia and Canada saw extreme measures taken, such as arresting people who do not wear masks and putting some in *Covid camps (6)*. Some countries made vaccines mandatory, such as Israel (7). The West no longer enjoyed the freedom they had due to totalitarian measures implemented through lockdowns and military style police forces. It no longer felt like democracy because in all honesty it was not! Fear, propaganda, and control ensured most people would obey the rules.

Satan's agenda is no longer hiding in the shadows, now it's being displayed openly to the world. The conditioning process for the implementation of the beast system is almost done, the world is almost ready for the beast to be unleashed. The word of God calls Gods people to expose the evil deeds of darkness (Ephesians 5:11). We are to be a light shining in this present darkness (Ephesians 5:7-14).

There is no need to fear the tribulation, for God will never leave us nor forsake us (Hebrews 13:5). The new world order is on the horizon, it is even being spoken about through leaders such as Joe Biden and events through the economic forum (8 & 9)! Yet, it is clear how the story really ends... The splendour of Gods coming will destroy Satan's earthly reign (2 Thessalonians 2:8), Those who are slain for their testimony of Christ will reign with Him for a thousand years (Revelation 20:4), the thousand years will be a time of true peace on earth! (Isaiah 11:6-9; 32:18). God can keep His people from falling (Jude 24-25). Jesus is preparing His bride for the arrival of the groom and soon His bride will be gathered for the great wedding feast of the lamb (Revelation 19:6.9) Do not be afraid! *There is no fear in love for true love expels all fear* (1 John

4:18). The people of God must spiritually separate themselves from the world and spread the good news of Jesus Christ; spend time in prayer, bible study and worship. This will equip the believer to be rooted and grounded in God with a firm foundation. When the storms come, they will stand strong for they have made themselves ready.

When Jesus said, *watch that no one deceives you* (Mark 13:5), he has endowed the people of God the responsibility to make sure they are not deceived. The way to avoid being deceived is to be filled with the truth found in God's word, this is how the believer is to keep watch.

Wars and rumours of war

Many military nations are amid an arms race, aiming to build up their military might to become a powerful army. Leaders love flaunting their military might through parades and weapon testing. China, North Korea, and Russia often have military parades to show the world their capabilities. Russia holds their annual victory day each year on the 9th of May. China held its 70th victory day parade on the 03/09/2015 (10), 70 years and 1 day after the end of World War 2. In September 2018 North Korea also had its 70th victory day parade since the beginning of the Jong families dynasty (11). These events are a harmless way for nations to show off military might and the latest technological advances concerning weapons, such as the ballistic missile.

Why do nations build up military power? There are two primary reasons... first, to defend their land, second, to attack someone else's or third, perhaps they just want to be powerful, and pride leads them to build it up. These supposedly harmless parades showcase an array of weapons that have the power to wipe out nations. When nations see these parades they are stirred to invest more money (debt money!) into funding weapons and military advancements.

Not all nations have a military, according to the *CIA world fact book (in 2019)* the world still has 36 nations/territories without a standing military. These 36 nations are; Andorra, Aruba, Cayman Islands, Cook Islands, Costa Rica, Curacao, Dominica, Falkland Islands, Faroe Islands, French Polynesia, Greenland, Grenada, Iceland, Kiribati, Kosovo, Liechtenstein, Macao (autonomous territory of China), Marshall Islands, Mauritius, Federated states of Micronesia, Monaco, Montserrat, Nauru, New Caledonia, Niue, Palau, Panama, St. Lucia, St. Vincent and the Grenadines, Samoa, San Marino, Sint Maarten, Solomon Islands, Svalbard (unincorporated region of Norway), Tuvalu and Vanuatu. These nations may still have police forces, but they see no need for a military as they are rarely targeted by more powerful nations.

Many nations have been involved in bloody historic battles, therefore, if they de-constructed their military they would become an easy target for old enemies. In our modern world, armies and weapons are so vast and powerful that they could destroy our beautiful marble planet many times over. We could obliterate ourselves with nuclear weapons. According to the website www.poughshares.com (world nuclear weapon stockpile) nine countries in the world possess a total of 13,850 nuclear weapons between them, 92% of them owned by Russia and the United States! This is a scary concept considering Russia's aggression in Ukraine and plans for taking more countries. God forbid that any nuclear weapons be used in our time! Humanity now has the power to destroy the earth, one nuclear bomb would set off a domino effect, hence why nobody wants to push that apocalyptic button. World superpowers know the dangers and have refrained from using them, but during the 21st century a hostile takeover has been happening on the world stage, only by the grace of God have such weapons not been used.

When Jesus spoke about wars and rumors of wars, he was speaking about multiple wars happening simultaneously around the world. The world has never seen such an array of conflicts until now. The Middle East has been a continuous battleground for conflicts ever since Jesus walked the earth and no doubt before. A historic peace plan has been recently drafted by Jared Kushner in a plan that Donald Trump has hailed as the deal of the century (12). According to scripture, when the Middle East has peace, then the tribulation is about to begin. To this day, daily conflicts continue to ravage the Middle East; Israel and Palestine continue to be hostile over the 2-state solution, Iran is close to developing a nuclear weapon – perhaps they even have one, Mahmoud Ahmadinejad once said that Israel must be wiped off the map (13) and Israel have threated retaliation if they build a nuclear weapon (14). Along with this, on the 6th December 2017, the USA recognized Jerusalem as the capital of Israel (15), this was like kicking a hornet's nest as the Palestinians and Muslims despised this. The Middle East is like a tinder box, a tiny spark could set off a war.

Consider the shear miracle of Israel's existence since it was born in a day on May 14th, 1948! Israel is a small land mass of only 22,072KM with a population of 8 and a half million according to the 2019 consensus. The nations surrounding Israel dwarf it by comparison, yet still surrounding nations have not succeeded in conquering Gods Holy land. Our eyes should be firmly kept on Israel during these end times. Wars are prophesied to happen according to Ezekiel 38 & 39, Zephaniah 1:1-11. This will be fulfilled with the Russia, Turkey and Iranian coalition that will one day attack Israel. This alliance was impossible until recent times, but since the war in Syria and the seizing of oil tankers in the Persian Gulf during the summer of 2019, this alliance has now been built (16). This alliance has been strengthening as military has been building up in Israel's neighboring country Syria. Iran and Russia became closer allies ever since the Trump administration abandoned the nuclear agreement in 2015 and crippled Iran's sales of oil for a time. Even though the Biden administration has re-built ties with Iran, the relationship with Russia and Iran remains.

Since 1948 Israel has suffered some conflicts, one of the most memorable was the 1967 six-day war. This war was fought between Israel and Arab nations such as, Egypt, Jordan and Syria who was partially helped by Iraq, Saudi Arabia, Kuwait, and Algeria (Wikipedia – wars of Israel since 1948). The odds were firmly stacked against Israel, yet still Israel won! Some could say this was due to

Israel's technology and strong military might, but Gods invisible hand was inevitably at work. No doubt Israel has some of the most advanced weapons on earth and the iron dome to deflect incoming missiles, but Israel stands today because God protects His chosen nation. Why are so many nations obsessed with destroying tiny land Israel? It is because the devil believes if He can destroy Israel as a nation then it will nullify the prophecies of scripture. The devil is doomed to fail, Israel will never be destroyed and will never be abandoned by God.

A different kind of war has been happening in modern times, the so-called war on terror that was initiated after the dreadful attacks on September the 11th 2001. This *war on terror* gave the green light for America to start sending troops into Iraq, Lebanon, and Syria. All these countries have unfortunately fell apart internally since this has happened, war begets war. The UK and other nations joined American forces. No doubt terrorism must be confronted, but unfortunately sending troops to these lands caused them to send more terrorists to ours.

Over the last 70 years multiple wars have broken out, perhaps more than any other time in history. Yet according to the words of Jesus, it is when multiple wars are happening at the same time for various reasons when we should be alert. America and many Western allies have a war on *racism and terror.* Syria and other nations have suffered civil wars that has internally destroyed their nations. African nations such as CAR, Sudan, Nigeria, Congo, Angola, Libya, Somali and many more have suffered wars! China and the USA have been in *trade wars* (17). China has threatened to invade Taiwan (18), Russia has invaded Ukraine and may invade other European countries and then eventually Israel. There are rumors of Cyber wars through cyber-attacks. Today war is not just on the battlefield with soldiers, war is through technology; against certain people groups, against certain ideologies, one day the war will be against the saints (Revelation

13:7). Yes, wars and rumors of wars are happening all the time, the words of Jesus are true and powerful.

Since the end of World War 2 the world has advanced rapidly bringing new and more dangerous weapons annually. Oh, how believers in God crave for the fulfilment of Gods words in Isaiah 2:4 *and he shall judge among the nations and rebuke many people; and they shall beat their swords into ploughshares and their spears into pruning hooks; nation shall not lift sword against another, neither shall they learn war anymore.* A day is coming when there will be no need for the military as true peace will rule the earth.

Kingdom against Kingdom

Ephesians 6:12 *For our struggle is not against flesh and blood, but against the rulers, against the authorities, against the powers of this dark world and against the spiritual forces of evil in the heavenly realms.*

The principles for Kingdom against Kingdom are different to wars and rumors of war; wars that Jesus mentioned are concerning the physical realm, Kingdom against Kingdom is concerning the spiritual. Before mankind was created Satan and God were already enemies. The devil rebelled against God and took one third of the angels with him (Revelation 12:3-4), he has also caused many humans to rebel. The earth has been ransacked, corrupted and run by the devil since the fall of mankind recorded in Genesis 3. Earth was a paradise before sin entered the scene, sinless humans walked with God as one walks with a friend. Paradise was lost because of sin, only to be restored again at the end of all things in the new heaven and new earth (Revelation 21).

Good and evil have been at war since the beginning, the intensity of the conflict has increased since Jesus sealed the victory by his death and resurrection. The world is caught up in the cross fires of this battle, but many have no clue about it. Two spiritual Kingdoms are fighting, the Kingdom of darkness and the Kingdom of light. Both Kingdoms operate on different values; one is eternal the other temporary, one brings freedom the other is controlling, one honors God and the other does not. These spiritual forces have been the driving force behind revivals and uprisings, healing and death, restoration and destruction, love, and hate.

The devils church

The devil's church does not necessarily mean the blatant worship of Satan through the Satanist cult founded by

Anton LaVey (19); he refers to them as worshippers of Satan or Luciferians. It does not mean other Satanic cults that are involved in detestable acts of child sacrifice and sexual exploitation, this rabbit hole is too deep to explore in this book. Though these groups are part of the devil's church, there is another cunning church that the devil also has formed. This deceptive church is the infiltration of false believers who have wormed their way into local churches overtime and corrupted the purity of the gospel. The infiltration tactic has been an attack against the Kingdom of God that has not just diluted the message of God or caused division but has also led people astray via meaningless distractions. Here is an example of the enemy's tactic, taken from C.S Lewis Screwtape letters – letter 2.

Mr. dear wormwood,

I note with grave displeasure that your patient has become a Christian. Do not indulge the hope that you will escape the usual penalties; indeed, in your better moments, I trust you would hardly wish to do so. In the meantime, we must make the best of the situation. There is no need to despair; hundreds of these adult converts have been reclaimed after a brief sojourn in the enemy's camp and are now with us. All the habits of the patient, both mental and bodily, are still in our favor. One of our greatest allies at present is the church itself. Do not misunderstand me. I do not mean the church as we have seen her spread out through all time and space rooted in eternity, terrible as an army with banners. That, I confess, is a spectacle which makes our boldest tempters uneasy. But fortunately, it is quite invisible to these humans... Make his mind flit to and fro between an expression like "the body of Christ" and the actual faces in the next pew... Work hard, then, on the disappointment or anti-climax which is certainly coming to the patient during his first few weeks as a churchman. The enemy allows the disappointment to occur on the threshold of every human endeavor. It occurs when the boy who has been enchanted in the nursery by stories from the Odyssey buckles down to really learning Greek. It occurs when lovers have got married and begin the real task of learning to live together. In every department of life, it marks the transition from dreaming aspiration to laborious doing. The enemy takes this risk because He has a curious fantasy of making all these disgusting little human vermin into what he calls "free" lovers and servants – "sons" is the word he uses, which His inveterate love of degrading the whole spiritual world by unnatural liaisons with the two-legged animals. Desiring their freedom, He refuses to carry them, by their mere affections and habits, to any of the goals he sets before them: He leaves them to "do it on their own". And there lies opportunity. But also, remember their lies danger. If once they get through this initial dryness successfully, they become much less dependent on emotion and therefore much harder to tempt...

This letter highlights how the enemy preys on distraction, disappointment, and dependency on emotions for the believer in Christ. The gospel does not always need to be diluted for one to be driven from faith; sometimes disappointment or distractions are enough to lead one astray. A Kingdom divided against itself cannot stand (Mark 3:24), the attack on disunifying the body of Christ has weakened part of the global church. The church does not have to succumb to the enemy's attacks! Resist the devil and he will flee (James 4:7) We resist by submitting ourselves fully to God.

The enemy will continue his onslaught until he is thrown into the bottomless pit (Revelation 20:3). The man of sin (the antichrist) will finalize the attacks when declaring war on the saints (Revelation 13:7). The climatic war of Kingdom against Kingdom will dominate the world during the final seven years before the return of Christ, especially the last 3 and a half of those tribulation years which is filled with intense persecution. Human power cannot destroy the antichrist. Christs splendor when He returns will destroy his power (2 Thessalonians 2:8).

The church must learn to take care of new believers to protect them from the deceptive ways of the enemy. Mature Christians have a significant role to play in discipling those new to the faith. Romans 15:1 *We who are strong in the faith should help the weak with their weakness, and not please only ourselves.* It is not just the preacher or the pastor who should help the weak, all of us who are stronger should be involved. The enemy prowls over the new believer just like a lion prowls over a newborn deer, easy to snatch if they are separated from the herd. God will unify His church in these last days, He will return for a bride ready to meet their groom.

The conversion illusion

During grand Christian festivals such as the Billy Graham crusades, countless people made a confession of faith unto Christ. Overwhelmed by the mountain top experience of God, they surrender their lives to Jesus. The people of God are filled with joy, angels rejoice for the one sinner who repents (Luke 15:10), and we gladly accept the newcomer. Some of these confessors grow in faith and eventually do great works for God, but many fall away once the cares of life or persecution arrive. Where has the church been going wrong for so many to fall away?

Every confessor of faith should be treated as genuine, but conversion needs to be followed up with discipleship. Jesus called us to make disciples of all nations (Matthew 28:19) not converts. When a new believer is left isolated to conjure up their own interpretation of the gospel, the devil is eagerly waiting so he can present his twisted version – this is where people like Joseph Smith start movements such as Mormonism (20). Those who know the word need to teach the new believer the ways of God.

Fake conversions do not bear fruit, they are those who make a spur of the moment commitment because everyone else is doing it. It takes time for fruit to grow on a tree, therefore fake conversions cannot be noticed in the beginning, time is required to see if one bears fruit. There are two types of fake conversions... the ones who do it because everyone else is, jumping on the band wagon as they say or, the ones who know they are not truly confessing and instead are serving the purposes of Satan or their own agenda. The devil doesn't mind a confession so long as its only with the lips and not also with the heart. Romans 10:9 *If you confess with your mouth Jesus is Lord **and** believe in your heart that God raised him from the dead, you will be saved* (emphasis added). It requires both confession and belief in the heart to ensure salvation. False confessors may be very diligent for the things of God such as outreach, organizing church events, attending bible study, and perhaps even praying to some extent. It is not a person's works that reveal a pretender, it is seeing whether the person develops the genuine fruit of the Spirit, which is love, joy, peace, patience, kindness, goodness, faithfulness, gentleness, and self-control (Galatians 5:22). Those who truly seek Jesus will desire Jesus more than His Kingdom and seek to grow in understanding and stature concerning the things of God. Pray for Gods discernment concerning this matter, He will reveal the truth.

Religion

Here is a shocking statement that many may not accept... *religion kills.* Religion does not only kill physically, but also spiritually, morally, and mentally. The reason for this is because of miss-applications of beliefs or extreme radical views. For example, the holocaust happened due to

23

propaganda teaching citizens to hate Jewish people (21). A term called anti-Semitism was already formed in the 1800s and still applies today when hatred is stirred towards the Jews (22). Other examples of religion kills are the crusades (23), Islamic extremism, communism, and underground discoveries of sexual exploitation by the priesthood of the catholic church (24). No doubt some good comes out of religions such as charitable deeds to help the poor and needy, but in some cases the good is overshadowed by a sinister evil, even in the name of Christianity.

Christianity is a religion, right? By stature Christianity is renown as a religion, by practice it is about relationship. Yet Christians have still made mistakes concerning miss-guided applications of the truth. The words of Jesus to *love our enemy* has sometimes been overridden by *eye for an eye and tooth for a tooth,* a rule implemented for judges during the Old Testament (Exodus 21:24) yet used by some to execute judgement on others. Christians are called to *turn the other cheek* (Matthew 5:39) and the Lord advises judgement is his, *it is mine to payback* (Romans 12:9). Playing the role of governor or God by executing judgement/punishment since the death and resurrection of Christ has nullified the power of the gospel. One may say, *how can Christianity be about love and forgiveness when many are killed in Christs name?* Here lies the danger of miss applying Gods word.

Religion is a powerful tool of the enemy because he can indoctrinate many with seemingly good principles while keeping them away from the infallible truths found only through Gods word. If Satan can disguise himself in the name of religion, then any miss-application can be attributed to God instead of him. This is a masterplan for keeping people away from the truth, but *with God all things are possible (Matthew 19:26)* many can still be saved despite this.

Religion in a sense is its own Kingdom because all religions believe in a God or a higher power along with certain principles, acclaimed truths and skewed images of immortal beings or eternal places. The world has thousands of religions, many are found in India alone (25). Yet with these thousands, none of them has been proven to be the fundamental truth. Christianity stands out because evidence has contributed to the belief such as the discovery of the dead sea scrolls between 1947-1956 (26). Not only has evidence been found but prophecies have also been fulfilled. Jesus fulfilled many Old Testament prophecies, such as Isaiah 53, many others have also been fulfilled since the resurrection, such as the birth of Israel as a nation, still, many more are being fulfilled today. The book of Daniel and Revelation has much to say about bible prophecy. Christianity has persevered the testing of time through persecution, apostasy, famines, wars, and many other calamities. The light of the church has not been snuffed out, Jesus said, *the gates of hell shall not prevail against the church* (Matthew 16:18). Many have scoffed at the bible to disprove its validity, one of the most famous of those scoffers was C.S. Lewis, an atheist that tried to disprove the bible only to end up believing in what is written.

Relationship not religion.

Christians adhere to the belief in a personal God found in Christ Jesus our Lord. Christianity is therefore based on a saving relationship with the God who came in flesh and died a sinner's death in the place of all who believe in Him. This separates Christianity from all other "religions" because it is completely personalized to individual belief. No other belief claims their God died for them, rose from the grave conquering death and thus making a way for eternal life. God refers to himself as the *living God* (Jeremiah 10:10). He is alive and active in the world and interaction with Him primarily takes place through prayer, bible study and worship. God holds infinite knowledge, wisdom and power and yet chooses to humbly approach our sinful dwelling. Gods of some religions only honor the strong; or can only be found through some strenuous self-discipline effort or require human sacrifices for their appeasement. Examples of such evil sacrifices were offered to Baal, Ashtoreth and Molech as found in the Old Testament. King Solomon rejected following God almighty to follow these Gods (1 Kings 11:4-11). The evil practice of human sacrifice was forbidden by God (Leviticus 20:2-5) as this is detestable to Him.

Relationship with the living God opens the deepest parts of the human soul. When a someone connects with the infinite God, God reforms that person into His image, for we were made in Gods image (Genesis 1:27). Relationship brings life, religion brings death. Jesus puts everything into a clear perspective when he said, *I am the way, the truth, and the life, no one comes to the father except through me* (John 10:10).

The Kingdom of darkness and light will continue to be in battle until Jesus Christ comes in power and glory, destroying the power of darkness in His glorious light. Satan knows he *has but a short time* (Revelation 12:12), evil will accelerate until the world is ripe for judgement. True Christians will be targeted because they stand for the truth and do not live for this world. Keep praying as a believer *thy Kingdom come, thy will be done* (Matthew 6:10), *Seek first the Kingdom of God* (Matthew 6:33) and fear not, *for Jesus has overcome the world* (John 16:33). Any believer in Christ who holds onto these truths and lives by them will not fall away.

Earthquakes

The website www.statista.com holds records of earthquakes, the number of earthquakes bigger than 5 on the Richter Scale have been skyrocketing since the year two thousand. Earthquakes are not a new phenomenon, but the scale and frequency of them are something to keep an eye on. Here is a chart of earthquakes higher than 5 between the years 2000 – 2017...

2000 – 1,505 earthquakes worldwide
2001 – 1,361 earthquakes worldwide
2002 – 1,341 earthquakes worldwide
2003 – 1,358 earthquakes worldwide
2004 – 1,672 earthquakes worldwide
2005 – 1,844 earthquakes worldwide
2006 – 1,865 earthquakes worldwide
2007 – 2,270 earthquakes worldwide
2008 – 1,948 earthquakes worldwide
2009 – 2,057 earthquakes worldwide
2010 – 2,383 earthquakes worldwide
2011 – 2,481 earthquakes worldwide
2012 – 1,523 earthquakes worldwide
2013 – 1,595 earthquakes worldwide
2014 – 1,729 earthquakes worldwide
2015 – 1,565 earthquakes worldwide
2016 – 1,696 earthquakes worldwide
2017 – 1,566 earthquakes worldwide

This amount of *felt* earthquakes is staggering, averaging between 3-5 times a day. Earthquakes in parts of the world such as *the pacific ring of fire* (Japan, Chile, Pacific Islands, West coast of America, Antarctica, Russia, Indonesia, and other countries nearby) are not uncommon as these countries are sitting on fault lines. However, Jesus said that earthquakes would be in diverse places, meaning places where earthquakes are unusual such as parts of Europe and Africa that do not have fault lines.

Jesus described earthquakes as a woman in labour; the closer the birth date becomes, the more intense the contractions. The world is contracting with more intensity as the end draws near with the tribulation and Christs return in sight. Scientists have attempted to attribute these earthquakes as a normal cycle the earth passes through, but intellectual minds are baffled with the sheer scale of earthquakes. Counting them all on the Richter Scale could reach at least 50, 000 a year, this is phenomenal. You will not hear of these numbers unless they happened to cause great destruction, like the tsunami that wreaked havoc on Japan's Honshu Island in 2011 after a 9.0 earthquake hit (27). Global leaders cannot blame climate change for earthquakes, no one except Christ can give a valid explanation.

The earth is groaning for restoration (Romans 8:22), for the earth has had her fill of blood ever since the murder of Abel. Gods people have a role to play when catastrophes like earthquakes happen, we are to be the hands and feet of Jesus offering help in times of distress. Many poor countries do not have the infrastructure to withstand the shaking, buildings collapse and people perish. All though earthquakes are largely unpredictable, just like tornados, buildings can be re-enforced, and nations better equipped to deal with such events. It would be wise for people not to live on major fault lines knowing that these areas are prone to great shakings. Seismologists have noticed that when clusters of earthquakes happen (such as in California or Yellow stone) then the likeliness of a bigger earthquake increases dramatically. However, despite this knowledge, the information is inconclusive as it has proved to not always be accurate. Nobody wants the super volcano at Yellow Stone to erupt as this would impact the whole Western hemisphere!

According to www.geology.com the biggest earthquake recorded was in 1960 near Valdivia in Southern Chile, its measure was a whopping 9.5 on the Richter Scale and lasted around 10 minutes! The damage and death toll were unprecedented. Magnitude 9+ is extremely rare, but when they happen the results are devastating. One day an earthquake will happen that causes *every mountain and island to be moved out of place* (Revelation 6:14) so great and powerful this earthquake that the *elites of the world run and try to hide in caves* (Revelation 6:15), this is during the time of Gods judgment. Earthquakes are a sign that the end of age is near, the more we see and the bigger they are, the closer we are to the Lords return.

Famines

A famine is a widespread scarcity of food, caused by several factors including war, inflation, crop failure, population imbalance, or government policies. Every inhabited continent in the world has experienced a time of famine through-out history. (Information Wikipedia)

It is a sobering topic to discuss famine in our modern Western society, but since Covid gripped the world, supply chains disrupted, inflation and war, the prospect of famine is far more likely. Before now, famine was only heard of in our modern age in places in Africa, the Middle East, some parts of Asia and South America, but now Europe could soon face famine. Weather plays a major role due to lack of rain, however another major role is war. Famine has affected the following war-torn countries, Sudan, Yemen, Nigeria, Syria, Venezuela and other South American, Middle East countries. War creates scarcity, looting leaves shops bare as desperation increases and this leaves behind a trail of devastation. Famine is not something new, but famines on such a scale as we see today have never been seen before in recent years. Perhaps during Old Testament times such famines happened, but the population of earth was much lower, so less people were impacted. The only good thing that comes out of famines is people turn to God to meet their needs.

Sometimes famines are a result of Gods judgments as found in Deuteronomy 28:48, Isaiah 3:1, Jeremiah 24:10 and Ezekiel 14:21. Other times famines are a result of sin and the curse that was placed upon earth in Genesis 3:17 after the fall. Still, other times are because of man's selfishness and wars. During these last days famines and earthquakes will be more common and happening simultaneously, along with wars, persecution, and lawlessness. A time is coming when *bread will cost a day's wages* (Revelation 6:6) *when people can only buy and sell with the mark of the beast* (Revelation 13:16,17). It seems this time is coming soon!

We have certainly seen a dress rehearsal of how all this might play out since Covid ravaged the world. Some countries made life hellish for the unvaccinated by creating vaccine passes to enter certain venues, for travelling and restaurants. Hatred was stirred towards the unvaccinated in which the flames were fanned by mainstream media. The hatred made no sense as the reason behind vaccinated people was meant to be so people could be protected; therefore, for the vaccinated to hate the unvaccinated made no sense if they believe they are protected.

Covid created a power vacuum to quickly be filled by totalitarian leaders seizing the opportunity for control. Through this pandemic many small companies were closed and rich companies such as Amazon and Facebook grew exponentially. Food prices rose as supply chains were systematically destroyed, Covid was used as the scapegoat.

War in Ukraine has pushed the world further into a cataclysmic reality. Who would have thought this would happen to the West in such a short period of time? Some could say these events seem to have been in the works for a long time. The *new world order* means the old-world order needs to be destroyed. Famine is now a very likely scenario on the world scene within a very short period. The next big hit, such as an economic crash, would be the final straw to usher in the new world order and the man of sin to lead this new world.

The believer need not fear the events that must take place. Jesus said in Matthew 4:4 *man shall not live on bread alone, but on every word that comes from the mouth of God.* Jesus was not abolishing physical food, but rather pointing to a far more sustainable food, a spiritual food through feasting on the word of God. Gods' words created the whole universe out of nothing. John 1:1-3 *In the beginning was the word, and the word was with God, and the word was God. The same was in the beginning with God. All things were made by Him, and without him was not anything made that was made.* The word of God is the eternal sustainable source for all people. Therefore, we are not without hope in this dark hour; anyone who trusts in God almighty can endure any circumstances. God does not live within this global system as we do, He is not bound by anything. Just as the Israelites were rescued from physical Egypt, the Lord will also rescue His people from Spiritual Egypt – the world we live in today. Gods people will be rescued from the land of slavery and led into the promised land. If people do not realize how they have become slaves to this new system, then perhaps answer the following questions. *Can I survive without money? How long can I go without my mobile phone? Can I imagine life without technology? Can I truly think for myself without asking Google for the answer? If this whole system collapsed, would I collapse with it?* Think about these questions.

God does not get a kick out of suffering and enjoy bringing judgement because of sin. God is long suffering so that many may turn and be saved, especially during times of trial and difficulty. The heart of our father in heaven is that many will repent and believe in His son Jesus Christ. Sometimes a great shaking must take place to strip away the security of people, it is there in the vulnerability of despair that they may find God. Until the last second, salvation is available to any who will turn to Christ.

Pestilence

All though pestilence is not referenced in Matthew 24:3-30 it is mentioned in Luke 21:11.

Pestilence definition: A fatal epidemic disease, especially bubonic plague.

The 10 worst plagues in recorded history are the following:

Plague Of Justinian (Byzantine Empire, 541 - 750) – an estimated 100 million people died from this plague.

Black Plague (Mostly Europe, 1346 To 1350) – around 50 million people died from this plague – 60 % of Europe's population died during this period as the virus had an 80% death rate!

HIV/AIDS (Worldwide, 1960- Present) – So far the estimated death toll from aids is around 39 million.

1918 Flu – 20 million deaths.

Modern Plague, 1894-1903 – 10 million deaths.

Asian Flu, 1957-1958 – 2 million deaths.

Sixth Cholera Pandemic, 1899-1923 – 1.5 million deaths

Russian Flu, 1889-1890 – 1 million deaths.

Hong Kong Flu, 1968-1969 – 1 million deaths

Fifth Cholera Pandemic, 1881-1896 – 981, 899 deaths.

Information (The 10 Worst Epidemics In History - WorldAtlas)

Since 2019 there has also been Covid, with an estimated 6 million deaths (as of May 2022) attributed to the disease.

Whether the numbers who have died are accurate is debatable, the point is, many pestilences have ravaged the earth and destroyed the lives of many. Jesus said pestilence will be in various places; and as per the list, they certainly are. Thankfully modern medicine has minimized the death toll, but still pandemics take the world by surprise and can wreak havoc. Covid, however, has raised many questions, such as, why have people been said to die *with* the disease and not *from* it? This alone indicates other attributes caused the death, but Covid was blamed.

Until the curse is removed due to the fall, sickness will always be something we need to face. The great promise is that one day there will be *no more death or mourning or pain – for the former things have passed away (Revelation 21:4).* Yet if Jesus could touch the lepers and heal them, if he could make the blind see and raise the dead, and if the church has demonstrated the same power in the name of Jesus since the church was born – then we have no reason to fear!

Increase in wickedness and the love of many turning cold

When a person or society is in such peril that morality ceases to exist, the outcome is wickedness. Wickedness is when evil is called good and good is called evil; the upside-down Kingdom ruled by darkness. Wickedness is when a person or society forgets God and rebels against him; it is when people are so puffed up with pride that all kinds of evil take place.

Galatians 5:19-21 *The acts of the flesh are obvious: sexual immorality, impurity, and debauchery; idolatry and witchcraft; hatred, discord, jealousy, fits of rage, selfish ambition, dissensions, factions, and envy; drunkenness, orgies, and the like. I warn you, as I did before, that those who live like this will not inherit the Kingdom of God.*

The acts of the flesh are an example of what happens within a Godless society. The devil thrives in the realm of wickedness because those who live this way bind themselves to the devil for wickedness is the devil's nature.

Examples of wickedness; Britain's knife crime epidemic (28), mass shootings in America (29), corrupt governments globally – especially in poor nations, the Chinese communist regime, divided nations over political issues, violent protests, young people lost in a world of drugs, gang warfare – especially in South American countries and some African nations, terrorism, domestic violence, homelessness because of extreme inflation and war, child abuse, rape, murders, the sex trade, pornography, forced labor and much more could be said! Wickedness has spread around the world like wildfire and without God there would be no moral compass, *people*

35

would do what they think is right in their own eyes (Judges 21:25).

The news is full of reports of wickedness, sometimes we are not even shocked by horrific stories due to being desensitized. Desensitization happens when people get used to seeing something evil so that it no longer bothers them. Example – the war in Syria was a shock in the beginning, but after a few months the next big story took over and this was all forgotten by many. War and suffering should never become something that does not upset us. Thousands killed, millions internally displaced, suffering children and crying widows should always pull-on human heart strings; if the pull is no longer there then this indicates a huge issue of the heart.

The love of many truly has grown cold due to the increase in wickedness. The love has grown cold because people have forgotten about the one who defines love because He is love. Some may be asking, *"where is this God of love? Why is He not doing anything about this evil? Does God approve of such wickedness?"*. God is not silent about wickedness. The cross of Jesus Christ was a public spectacle so that all could see the atrocity of evil and the good that overcame it. God was not silent in the face of such evil; Jesus cried out *father forgive them* (Luke 23:34) while on the cross. God is moving in the world in mighty ways through dreams, visions, miracles, and restoration – but you will rarely find those stories on the mainstream platforms.

Some believers have fallen due to wondering where God is during such chaos, forgetting the promises of Christ that have been sealed by His blood. This generation should utter the same words of Esther, *we were born for such a time as this* (Esther 4:14). Those who believe in Jesus are called to be a light in this present darkness, a voice speaking up for those who are not heard, feet that bring good news and hands that help the poor. Those whose lives aim to please God change the world around them because they invite God into the circumstances. God will not force His way into the lives of those who want to live without him, they are free to choose. Yet the natural consequences of wanting a life without the creator of life is to end up spending eternity without Him.

Here are some examples of modern-day wickedness that have swept the world...

Acceptance of abortion – the value of human life from the world vs the value of human life from God.

*How **some** people see human life...*

According to the 2019 report on www.worldpopulationreview.com (abortion), there are 26 countries where abortions for any reason are illegal. Another 37 countries ban abortions unless the life of the mother is in danger. Still, many nations have legalized abortions and the leading nations are the USA and Russia. Those who consider the moment of conception the beginning of life opposes abortions, all though they may support abortions for such cases of rape, incest or if the mother's life is in danger. However, most abortions today have nothing do with such cases, but instead is hailed as; *"my body my choice"* or *"women's rights"*. These two controversial views have stirred up conflict in the abortion arena, especially when considering the right of the child who is in the womb. In some American states where the right for abortions have been in jeopardy, mass protests were held endeavouring to keep abortions as a women's right to choose.

There is hope for those who have had abortions or those who have performed them. God is merciful and will forgive the offender who sincerely asks forgiveness. There are circumstances where abortion is more understandable such as rape and incest – like when someone who is starving steals food, but forgiveness is still required from God. In such circumstances wisdom is required to make the best decision for the benefit of the mother and the child. Many people out there would love to foster or adopt the child if the mother cannot cope and does not want to abort the life within them. All steps should be taken to ensure the protection of human life, if a child can be spared from abortion then the child should be protected.

Isaiah 5:20 *Woe unto them that call evil good and good evil; that put darkness for light, and light for darkness; that put bitter for sweet and sweet for bitter.* The abortion pandemic that has swept the world has nothing to do with the protection of the mother's life, but instead is evil disguised as good. Calling the right to terminate life a *woman's right* or *my body my choice* is a sadistic move of the devil. Women have rights in many areas and yes it is the woman's body, but once the baby takes form and the heartbeat of another life is within that body, the body is now two bodies; so, it cannot be just the woman's right. Also, if the abortion is only a woman's right then what about the following; *Where is the man who made you pregnant? Where was your right when you gave your body freely to another man? When a thousand women show up to protest (some who are very young) why is there no men? Does a father not have a voice in this matter, or have they deserted the mother? Why not use protection to spare from pregnancy?*

It is obvious when looking deeper into the modern abortion craze that the origin is demonic. Satan has no issues taking innocent babies lives; He once inspired King Herod to kill baby Jesus, but God intervened. Babies are the future, without having them then there is no future, we would be like those in the classic film *children of men.* Since the abortion process began in 1973 millions of futures have been terminated; millions of children created in the image of God that never had a chance of life. If the world did not have 7 billion people but rather 70 million (around the population of Britain) then human life would be far more valued. Imagine you have a bag of M&M chocolates, when you have a full packet you do not appreciate the chocolate as much as when you have just a few left... this is how some people treat human life! God does not treat us this way, each creation unique and loved deeply by our heavenly father. Evil is self-destructive if there is no good for it to thrive from.

*How **God** sees human life...*

Jeremiah 1:5 *Before I formed you in the womb, I knew you, before you were born, I set you apart; I appointed you as a prophet to the nations.*

God knows us, even before we are born! God already knows the plans he has for us. Sure, sin can disrupt Gods individual plans or make the journey longer to the promised land, like the Israelites in the wilderness. However, Gods overall sovereign plan will always be achieved and cannot be thwarted by human will or the devil.

Psalm 139:13 *For you created my inmost being, you knit me together in my mother's womb.*

The thought of being knitted together forms a picture of a loving God who takes his time to carefully weave the fabrics of our being into form. Our inmost being was already created before we could see, walk, and talk! This is Gods depth of love for humanity. We cannot even grasp the depths of this love and how much Gods heart breaks over the loss of one innocent baby. Parents who love their children will have partial understanding, but it still does not compare. Imagine this feeling spanning over many years for the loss of millions of Gods beautiful children, Gods cup of wrath is surely filling up.

Gods principles are completely different to Satan's. God uniquely and unconditionally loves all he has made. Satan does not love, for that is impossible for Him. Satan's depopulation agenda is playing out in plain sight hidden under the banner of *women's rights.* God is merciful, but judgement will commence one day, for the cry of the blood of the innocent reaches up to heaven.

Homosexuality... The worlds view on our sexuality and human identity vs Gods view.

This is a hot potato topic that many professing Christians would rather avoid than discuss, but sooner or later we must confront this. Homosexuality has been celebrated over the last few years in array of colours, people who stand against it are now ostracized, ridiculed, and persecuted. Christian responses have varied from some saying, *"you will burn in hell"* or *"God hates gay people",* others have joined the parades insisting that God approves such practices. Others have remained silent on the issue out of respect or fear of backlash and still others, like a scene a few years ago in the Philippines, went out with signs saying, *"I'm sorry"* and *"Jesus didn't turn away and neither will we"* (30).

Are any of these approaches correct? How should a bible believing Christian who believes that sexual union is between husband and wife respond to this? The collective body of Christ have still not got the response right. Standing with signs of condemnation will push a person further away from God rather than drawing them near, it does not invite a person to come to Jesus Christ who can bring freedom. Supporting gay pride as a Christian does not align with the word of God concerning the matter and remaining silent due to fear is cowardice; yet if we do speak we speak in love. Finally, approaching with apologetic signs and saying *Jesus didn't turn people away* could miss-lead people and appear that the bible is advocating homosexuality. The church is in danger of compromise if the church does not stand for the truth, but again, it must be done with love. No doubt Christians who have condemned someone who is practicing homosexuality should repent as Jesus commanded for His people to love their neighbour. Satan would love nothing more than to deceive Gods people of doing a service to God by sharing *love* when really they are compromising their faith and the truth. Wisdom is needed from God for each circumstance.

It is true that Jesus did not turn anyone away, but still he said at times, *go and sin no more* (John 5:14, John 8:11). Jesus invites all people to himself; we are never too messed up to turn to Christ for *when we were Gods enemies Christ died for us* (Romans 5:10). The church should approach those practicing homosexuality with grace and truth, just as Jesus did. Condemnation does not bring repentance, but only pushes someone further away from God... God desires them to be saved! It is conviction stirred up by the Holy Spirit that will enable a person to repent and come to Christ. God can surely set them free and turn their life around, *is anything too hard for the Lord?* (Genesis 18:14).

What does the word of God say about homosexuality? What is Gods remedy?

Old Testament bible verses.

Leviticus 18:22 *You shall not lie with a male as with a woman; it is an abomination*

Leviticus 20:13 *If a man lies with a male as with a woman, both have committed an abomination; they shall surely be put to death; their blood is upon them.*

41

Sodom and Gomorrah were examples of judgement once a sinful city is beyond the ability to repent. These cities were destroyed by fire, but before judgement Abraham had a conversation with God. In Genesis 18:16-33 we find that God would have spared the city even for one righteous person. One of the sins rampant in these two cities was homosexuality. Jude 7 *Just as Sodom and Gomorrah and surrounding cities, which likewise indulged in sexual immorality and pursued unnatural desire, serve as an example by undergoing punishment of eternal fire.* Wickedness has a full measure and then judgement swiftly comes, God gives plenty of time for repentance. Not many like to mention Gods judgement, we would rather speak about baby Jesus than the righteous judge of the universe. Yet God is holy, and sin must be punished, if punishment was not required by God, then Jesus would not have endured the cross.

New Testament verses

Romans 1:26 *Because of this, God gave them over to shameful lusts. Even their woman exchanged natural sexual relations for unnatural ones. In the same way the men also abandoned natural relations with women and were inflamed for lust for one another. Men committed shameful acts with other men and received in themselves the due penalty of their error.*

If God gave them over does this mean He caused them to commit the act? If God gave them over this means the desire was already there and being pursued. The reason God gave them over is found in Romans 1:21-23 *For all though they knew God, they neither glorify him as God nor gave thanks to him, but their thinking became futile, and their foolish hearts were darkened. Although they claimed to be wise, they became fools and exchanged the glory of the immortal God for images made to look like a mortal human being and birds and animals and reptiles.* Pushing

God away opened the door for all kind of evil to come in, pushing God out of one's life gives plenty of room for the devil to move in.

Gods remedy
Romans 3:23 *For all have sinned and fall short of the glory of God.* This, therefore, includes the person who stole someone's pen at work to someone practicing homosexuality, both acts fall short of the glory of God. Romans 5:8 *But God demonstrated his own love for us in this: While we were still sinners Christ died for us.* God did not wait for humanity to fix itself before giving his life for us, instead, God gave his life amid all our sinning.

1 John 1:9 *If we confess our sins, he is faithful and just to forgive us our sins and to cleanse us from all unrighteousness.* God will forgive any sinner who sincerely repents. Those who repent and turn to Christ *become a new creation, the old has gone and the new has come (2 Corinthians 5:17).* Those who have been deeply rooted in sinful behaviors may need extra help and support from fellow believers, the church should be ready to help and be patient with newcomers. God is faithful even when we are not (2 Timothy 2:13), God will also finish what he started concerning our faith journey (Philippians 1:6).

The remedy is found in Christ alone. Many realize that homosexuality is not Gods original design for sex because God has given a conscience to those he created. This means that many are choosing to rebel against Gods ways and do not want him to interfere with their lives. The whole world is captured in rebellion to God, for *Satan has blinded the minds of those who do not believe in Christ (2 Corinthians 4:4).* God waits patiently for anyone who is willing to repent, but the time of grace is almost up, and judgement will soon commence. The plead of God for all people today is... *today is the day of salvation (2 Corinthians 6:2)*

Transgenderism

Definition – *Denoting or relating to a person whose sense of personal identity and gender does not correspond with their birth sex.* The technology for changing a person's sex was non-existent until the year 1930. In 1930, the first realignment surgery (sex change) was undertaken, and the participant was changed from male to female (31). Sex changing technology advanced from then on and the amount of people changing sex increased dramatically.

Instead of discussing the procedures technicalities, let's look at the mindset behind the ones pursuing a sex change. The mind is a powerful God given tool that can be used for great or evil purposes. As one thinks so they become. Strongholds are built through repetitive thinking about the same thing over and over. For example: If a person continually thinks they are a loser or a failure and will never be good at anything, eventually this thought will be evident in the person's life. A person who thinks about rejection creates rejection, then they continue to think they are always rejected; sometimes they then reject others for fear of being rejected – this is the power of the mind effecting a person's actions. This kind of mindset can lead people into deep depression and in worst cases suicide – the mind is extremely powerful! It works the same way for good things, for the one who says *I can do it!* They will push until what they want to do is achieved.

A stronghold developed during childhood is extremely difficult to demolish because of how deeply ingrained it is. Seeds are sown into the minds of children; these seeds are watered and grow with repetitive thinking. This is where the seeds of *lies* can be planted into an innocent mind that some may begin to believe is the truth. A lie such as an anorexic person believing they are fat all though they obviously are not. Studies conclude that people who believe they are anorexic believe this because they think that's how they look.

Many who think they are born into the wrong body have seeds planted at a young age, seeds of doubt and confusion. The belief is solidified when the body forms into an image that is different to what they believe. This is when the individual thinks something is wrong and searches for a solution, and this is where new technologies come in. The transgender issue is not always the individuals mindset, sometimes external forces play a role in the development of this belief.

The following story is a snippet taken from www.USAtoday.com – OPINION Hormones, surgery, regret: *I was a transgender woman for 8 years – time I can't get back.*

I started my transgender journey as a 4-year-old boy when my grandmother repeatedly, over several years, cross-dressed m in a full-length purple dress she made especially for me and told me how pretty I was as a girl. This planted the seed of gender confusion and led to my transitioning at age 42 to transgender female.

I lived as "Laura" for 8 years, but, as I now know, transitioning doesn't fix the underlying ailments.

Studies show that most people who want to live as the opposite sex have other psychological issues, such as depression or anxiety. In my case, I was diagnosed at age 40 with gender dysphoria and at age 50 with psychological issues due to childhood trauma.

Stories of regret have been told from people who transitioned, they regret it because it did not fix the underlying issue (32).

Drag Queens

A shocking move of the 21st century is the mass acceptance of transgenderism and drag queens. In the USA and UK, drag queens have been able to perform in schools and public libraries, influencing children at a very young age and in some cases without parental consent. It is not only Christian and Muslim parents in opposition to this, but many nonfaith based families oppose such a move. On the flip side, some parents see this as an expression of love and freedom.

A story found on WWW.lifesitenews.com describes a drag queen known as "mama G", teaching kids how to twerk in a UK library! If you are not familiar with twerk/twerking, it is a style of dance known to be sexual and explicit. If the drag queen was not dressed up and such a performance was done by someone in normal clothes, there would be outrage and demands to arrest them. Yet when someone slaps on some women's clothes, a nice wig, tell jokes and act in ways that many women would not act, they can get away with it... most of the time. Societies have fallen to the point of approving such behaviors when the perpetrator is masked with comical props or a funny countenance. In this case with *mama G,* many opposed the outrageous act and said enough is enough. The library reported that they are committed to be *welcoming and inclusive for all,* but they will do a *police check on mama G.*

Drag queens were once viewed as people who want to have fun, dress up as a woman for a bit and tell some jokes. In modern times, the fun is being seen as something more sinister as the influence of some drag queens has indoctrinated children. A man dressing as a woman is his choice, but that man has no right to impose that choice on the minds of innocent children. Wanting to act as the opposite sex is usually a sign of a psychological issue but imposing that choice on anyone else can create more psychological issues. Children being taught that they must accept this behavior or perhaps becoming confused because of it, is not right. The consequences of teaching children to accept this as normal can have dire consequences once they grow up.

Believers in Christ need to be the moral voice speaking up for their generation according to the word of God. What is accepted as normal changes when society has no moral compass to direct them. The world and its ways may change but the word of God remains, for *God is the same yesterday, today and forever* (Hebrews 13:8). God is patient, not willing for any to perish and giving everyone time to come to him and be saved.

What does the bible say concerning these issues? The bible does not specifically say, *you should not change sex,* or *they were confused about their sex.* This does not mean the issue is not in in the bible because the issue is much deeper than physical appearance.

First, God made it very clear the sex of people that was made.

Genesis 1:27 *God created mankind in his own image, in the image of God he created them, **male** and **female** he created them.*
Genesis 5:2 *He created them **male** and **female** and blessed them.* In Genesis the emphasis of being made male and female was written twice, God was making a statement from the beginning.

Second, our thinking according to the word of God, is very important and has the power to change our lives.

Romans 12:2 *Do not conform to the pattern of this world but be transformed by the renewing of your mind. Then you will be able to test and approve what Gods will is – his good, pleasing, and perfect will.*

47

Philippians 4:8 *Finally, dear brothers and sisters, whatever is true, whatever is noble, whatever is right, whatever is pure, whatever is lovely, whatever is admirable, if anything is excellent or praiseworthy – think about such things.*

2 Corinthians 10:5 *We demolish arguments and every pretension that sets itself up against the knowledge of God, and we take captive every thought to make it obedient to Christ.*

Anyone who believes they were born in the wrong body are not without hope. Nobody is born in the wrong body, all though in rare circumstances one may be born without male or female sexual organs, but this is different to strongholds in the mind. Gods power can destroy strongholds of the mind and His word can renew the mind daily to enable a person to enjoy living in the body God gave them. Daily discipline of thinking about what we are thinking about will enable the mind to be strengthened and bring our thoughts and actions in line with the word of God. It is not impossible for the transgender or drag queen person to be restored. God loves them, Jesus Christ died for them as well as dying for Mother Theresa. They are not without hope and they must be told this good news.

Transhumanism

The term transhumanism was first coined in the 1960s as a word describing the transformation from man/woman into a machine or something that has supreme capabilities that far surpass that of humans. Think of films such as Robocop, X-men, Lucy or limitless, marvel films and so on – these give you glimpses of superhuman capabilities promised from leaders of the transhumanistic agenda. Modern films have been smothered by transhumanistic ideas that in our modern technocratic society do not seem so farfetched. Professors, scientists, and tech giants have meddled with this idea for years and now seem to be bringing ideas into a reality. Companies such as Tesla, Boston dynamics, deep mind and meta platforms are bringing sci-fi level AI into a reality. People such as Yuval Noah Harari believe that humans are soon entering the next phase of evolution where they will no longer be humans. These ideas and ambitions originate from the devil not God and are rooted in pride and rebellion – humans want to be more like God following the same footsteps as the devil.

No doubt the idea of transhumanism will be presented in a neat package of how beneficial it can be for humanity. For example: a human/machine could be made fireproof and rescue people from fires; or we could create iron man type super cops to fight crime and so on. The possibilities are endless but so are the dangers. Imagine this kind of technology in the wrong hands; if terrorists could be super villains and access data that could destroy the lives of many. Perhaps this technology is already in the wrong hands?

Transhumanism will be an invitation for the vulnerable and power-hungry people. If those who believe this is the next phase of evolution can make people despise being human, it will be easier to usher in this new demonic phase. Vulnerable people will accept the new phase simply because they are not satisfied with who they are; power-hungry people will look to advance themselves with technology for selfish purposes. After all, not many will refuse an opportunity to become smarter, stronger, and perhaps live for much longer if they are offered an *upgrade*. However, those who believe humans are created in Gods image will (or should) oppose such a move because there is nothing greater than being made in Gods image. Perhaps part of the reason for the future *war on the saints* is because true believers will be a testimony of the truth found in God's word and will not back down, no matter what the enemy throws at them.

There is no doubt that technology has its perks and is a great tool for so much, but the continued advancement is creating a technocratic society that is a dictator's menacing dream. The control over the lives of people is now beyond anything ever achieved in history. Chinas dystopian social credit score system for example (33), is like a snippet from George Orwell's novel *1984*. The global roll out of 5G provides the power required for such a power grid of control to exist – *the internet of things*, as they call it, perhaps one day those *things* will include humans.

The power of Gods Holy Spirit

If believers in Jesus Christ are tempted by the idea of becoming more than human, bear this in mind... *He who is in you is greater than he who is in the world* - 1 John 4:4. There is no greater power the world can offer than the power God has already gifted those who believe, the power of the Holy Spirit. The Holy Spirit within us is greater than the powers of the devil who seeks the destruction of humanity. Consider what has been accomplished by the power of the Holy Spirit; Jesus Christ was raised to life, the church was born, countless Christians have been emboldened to face torture and death, millions have been set free from the devil's bondage, communities and even nations have been restored to glory, multitudes of Muslims have turned to Jesus Christ and the list goes on! The reason the church may appear weak is because Gods people are trying to accomplish Kingdom work in their own strength. Jesus said he will *send the helper (John 15:26),* the helper will bring us to victory!

There is a huge problem when Gods church become numb or desensitized to the pain and suffering in this world. When a child of God is no longer broken for the things that break Gods heart then there is something deeply wrong. For the one who does not empathize anymore as Jesus did, they can surely be restored! The believer can spend intimate time with God and pray as Kind David prayed, *create in me a pure heart, O God, and renew a steadfast spirit within me. Do not cast me from your presence or take your Holy Spirit from me. Restore me to the joy of your salvation and grant me a willing Spirit to sustain me* (Psalm 51:10-12). The evil that is rampant in this world is the overflow of men's hearts, Covid was a great revealer of what's hidden within people's hearts. Therefore, it is imperative that we ask God to create a pure heart within us, one that reflects His. Clean hearts create pure words, and pure words produce better actions, and better actions make greater changes.

For out of the abundance of the heart the mouth speaks (Matthew 12:34)

Keep your heart with vigilance, for from it flow the springs of life (Proverbs 4:23).

Fools say in their hearts, "there is no God". They are corrupt, they do abominable deeds; there is no one who does good (Psalm 14:1)

Our hearts play a vital role not just in keeping our physical being alive, but also our emotional being. Only God almighty can reach into the dusty chasms of our hearts and cleanse the deepest parts of our being. Humans can clean up their act to a certain extent, but only God can clean the heart. May all believers declare the same words as Kind David in this sinful generation, *Create in me a pure heart, O God – amen.*

Persecution

All though persecution has been briefly mentioned, let's take a deeper look. There is nothing new about persecution, prophets of old were persecuted, the son of God was persecuted and so is the church. In fact, persecution should not take a Christian by surprise as *all who want to live a Godly life in Christ Jesus will be persecuted* (2 Timothy 3:12). Persecution stormed the early church like a flood, and this resulted in a rapid spread of the gospel, and many being saved. If those in modern Western society believe they will be raptured before enduring persecution, perhaps they need to look at church history.

On www.Christianitytoday.com (persecution in the early church) it describes how Christians endured 300 years of persecution from the Roman Empire. Early Christians considered suffering for their faith to be a great honor as it was following the footsteps of Christ who endured the cross. 1 Peter 4:16 *If you suffer as a Christian, do not be ashamed, but praise God that you bear His name.* The Roman governor of Bithynia did not hesitate to send anyone associated with being a Christian to be executed. Jews also persecuted the early Christians as they did not see Christianity as a reflection of the same God they believed in. Karl Barth, who was a theologian who wrote the epistle of the Romans said, *"the resurrection has proved its power, there are Christians – even in Rome".*

Gods power was great at work during persecution. Nero inflicted much suffering on Christians between 64-68 AD, Trajan also persecuted any who did not worship the emperor and Gods, Diocletian and Galerius began to imprison Christians until it escalated to immediate execution if they would not sacrifice to Roman Gods (34). Persecution in history is extensive, yet intense persecution continues to this day in place such as some

African countries, Middle East countries, North Korea, and China – where being a Christian carries a great cost. Yet, in places with extreme persecution the gospel is spreading like wildfire and Christians are as bold as lions. Persecution creates Kingdom warriors and weeds out worldly worriers.

Persecution takes away the middle ground of sitting on the fence half in and out for Jesus. Luke warmness cannot exist when the pressure of persecution lays heavily upon the believer. A choice is presented... *Do we compromise our faith so life can be easier? Or do we commit whole heartedly to the Lord and trust in His strength to endure?* Quote from a Middle Eastern Christian woman... *"Don't pray for the persecution to be stopped. ... But pray for the Christians there, for their boldness, their encouragement, for their faith and that they can all be witnesses for God's work and for God"(35).* Western civilization has enjoyed a prolonged period of peace with the USA as the world superpower, facing death for what we believe in is almost unheard of. Yet how long before we must endure the same way our brothers and sisters around the world do? In countries such as Syria, Nigeria, North Korea, Myanmar and China, Christians have suffered for what they believe in and some have lost everything, yet they *gain everything in Christ* (Philippians 3:8). Christian organizations such as Open Doors and Barnabus Fund have been registering persecutions for years and the many miracles that happen amidst the persecuting. Christians do not compromise because they understand that what is gained in Christ far outweighs what is lost on earth. *I consider that our present sufferings are not worth comparing with the glory that will be revealed in us. – Romans 8:18*

Why are Christians persecuted? Living the Christian life is counter cultural because it goes against what is considered the norm. When Christians do the following then some persecution or opposition is likely;

Wait until marriage for sex, love their enemies, don't retaliate when hurt by others, praises God even when things are difficult, is always thankful, loves their neighbor, reads, and believes the bible, worships the living God, stands against injustice and corruption, and always prays and speaks the truth... When Christians shine the light of Christ by living this way they may be marginalized by society because they are *different.* Worshipping the true living God really ruffles the feathers of Satan because he desires our worship and attention, and he will steal and kill to get it. Ultimately, Satan is behind persecution, for he stirs hatred in the Spiritual realm that manifests into the physical. Satan is the God of this world all though Jesus has supreme authority (Matthew 28:18) the world still reflects more of Satan's image than Gods and until Christ establishes his thousand-year reign Satan still holds great power and influence.

Why does God allow persecution? *Remember what I told you: "a servant is not greater than his master". If they persecuted me, they will persecute you also. If they obeyed my teaching, they will obey yours also (John 15:20).* Christ set an example to follow, and this includes a road marked with suffering. *If indeed we share in his sufferings in order that we may also share in his glory (Romans 8:17).* Persecution brings great glory to God on earth and future glory for the believer at the resurrection. The name of Jesus Christ is exalted highest when a believer remains faithful in the face of physical death.

Another reason for persecution is so those who are persecuting can hear the gospel message and receive salvation. The story in Acts 16:25-40 is a great example of a persecutor finding faith in Christ. Jesus warned in Matthew 10:18 *On my account you will be brought before Governors and Kings as witnesses to them and the gentiles.* Gods desire is for all to be saved, sometimes the only way some can hear the gospel is by arresting the ones who testify about it. Persecution also weeds off false believers, separating the sheep from the goats. Persecution purges the church of false prophets, false teachers, and false church goers. Those who use the name of Jesus for selfish, political or any other wrong motive will not last when persecution comes, unless they truly repent and are filled with the Holy Spirit.

Persecution is not something to fear but rather embrace. For those who fear physical suffering it is important to remember that endurance is because of Gods power and His Holy Spirit. Any who endure persecution do not focus on the temporary discomfort or pain, but rather on the eternal joy and glory to be revealed, this is how Jesus endured the cross. *Fixing our eyes on Jesus, the pioneer and perfecter of our faith. For the joy set before him he endured the cross, scorning its shame, and sat down at the right hand of the throne of God (Hebrews 12:2).* Persecution is coming to the West, whether we want to admit that or not we must face the truth of God's word about the arrival of the antichrist and the war on the saints. We cannot keep hoping that the moment persecution comes we will be raptured out of here before any suffering; saints in many parts of the world have not been raptured and for some of them they are in great tribulation. If Jesus is the author and perfector of our faith then we must allow him to build our faith in Him until we are unshakable concerning the Kingdom of God. Peace is found in Christ not our circumstances, *Peace I leave with you; my peace I give you. I do not give to you as the world gives. Do not let your hearts be troubled and do not be afraid (John 14:27).* Now is not the time for fear, it is the time for faith.

The preaching of the gospel

Through the internet, travel, and technological advances the gospel has been enabled to spread at lightning speed. Once upon a time news was only heard days or perhaps weeks after the event, but now news is just a click of a button away. Bibles and bible apps have been translated into multiple languages, missionaries have been sent via planes to mission lands, GOD TV has broadcast to millions around the world, and many are being saved! Yet still, even though the gospel has gone out into all the world, there is an estimated one billion people who have little or no knowledge of Jesus Christ, there is still so many people to share the good news with! Jesus endowed his church with the great co-mission, *to preach the gospel and make disciples of all nations (Matthew 28:19-20).* The sharing of the gospel is one of the greatest end time prophecies to be fulfilled.

    The preaching of the gospel is not determined by how many respond to the message but how many hear it. Jesus preached to many and yet many rejected His teaching, but his teaching was then a testimony against them if they chose not to accept the truth. *"they may be ever seeing but never perceiving, and ever hearing but never understanding; otherwise, they might turn and be forgiven!"* (Mark 4:12). The preaching of the gospel is required with or without a response from those who hear it, our mission is to be faithful. Anyone who has heard the truth of the gospel yet refuses to acknowledge the truth will be accountable to God and the preacher has done what was required.

Romans 10:14-17 *How then will they call on him in whom they have not believed? And how are they to believe in him of whom they have never heard? And how are they to hear without someone preaching? And how are they to preach unless they are sent? As it is written, "How beautiful are the feet of those who preach good news!"*

But they have not all obeyed the gospel. For Isaiah says, "Lord, who has believed what he has heard from us? "So, faith comes by hearing, and hearing through the word of Christ".

Hearing through the word of God enables faith, the message of Christ is powerful and will *not return to God void but will accomplish all God desires* (Isaiah 55:11). Those who reject God pre-determine a life without God, all though this hurts God He gives the freedom to live without him if this is truly what they want. Therefore, any who reject God once He is revealed to them cannot spend eternity with God, for God is giving them what they desire... a life without Him. All Christians are witnesses and share the same authority of the gospel for *all authority in heaven and earth was given to Christ. John the Baptist testified about Jesus in the wilderness* (John 1:19-34). Christians hold the testimony that *Christ died, Christ rose, and that Christ will come again* (Luke 24:46-47). This is the testimony of the church to the world, the sooner the message reaches those other one billion souls, the sooner this prophecy will be fulfilled.

The falling away

The Spirit clearly says that in the later times some will abandon the faith and follow deceiving spirits and things taught by demons. Such teachings come through hypocritical liars, whose consciences have been seared with a hot iron – Timothy 4:1-2.

The Greek word used in this passage is apostasia and this refers to a *deflection from the truth.* Therefore, the falling away can be understood as those who turn from the biblical truth and pursue other teachings. When prominent members of the church fall away it hurts the body of Christ and this can be difficult to comprehend. Since the birth of the church many have fallen away, but today those renouncing their faith is sadly a common occurrence. The famous author Joshua Harris publicly renounced his faith (36), so has Marty Sampson (37) and many others whose names may be recognised. Jesus warned about this falling away in Matthew 24:10 and that the man of sin (the antichrist) will not appear until the great falling away takes place. How can the man of sin enter the world stage if nobody will accept His lies and deceitful wonders? Many must turn from the truth before the antichrist is revealed, otherwise he will not have his moment of victory. Christians must continue to renew their faith daily and pursue Christ, the lifestyle of the Christian is a marathon not a sprint.

There are many reasons for why someone falls away from the truth. The parable of the sower in Matthew 13:1-23 provides an outline of three main reasons. These three reasons are as follows...

1) *Those who hear the word but do not understand because the devil steals what has been sown in the heart. This* example is the seed the fell on the path.

2) *Those who receive the word with joy but have no root so fade away after a short period when trials or persecution*

commence. This example is the seed sown on the rocky ground.

3) *Those who hear the word but are choked because of life's worries.* This example is the seed sown among the thorns.

These are the three reasons for why one falls, but there is one reason for those who do not fall. This is, *those who hear the word and understand, they hear the word and endure* – This example is the seed sown on the good soil.

Hard times reveal where the seeds have been sown into the believers life. When a renown believer who is well known suddenly confesses that they no longer believe, this is starting to those who know them or knew of them. Questions are raised such as, *why are they only saying this now? What triggered this confession? Were they genuine when they first believed?* Only God knows the heart and the depth of the reason, but no doubt this is concerning, and we should pray for them! When Satan requested for Peter to be sifted like wheat, *Jesus prayed for him, that his faith would not fail* (Luke 22:31-32). *We have a high priest who intercedes for us from heaven and can empathize with our weaknesses* (Hebrews 4:15). *For it is not the will of God that any who the father has given should be lost and that they should be raised up at the last day* (John 6:39). All true believers will be saved because the author and perfector of one's faith is Christ (Hebrews 12:2) and God is faithful, He will finish the good work he started. Faith is in the hands of God, not men, so we can be sure God knows what He is doing.

The story of the prodigal son in Luke 15:11-32 is a perfect illustration of the restoration of someone who fell away. The father could have overpowered the son and stopped him from squandering his inheritance. Yet, the father allowed the son to choose a sinful lifestyle despite the great love and concern he had for him. *Does the father not love his son for giving him freedom to choose?* It would be more menacing for the father to keep his son

59

on lockdown and not allow him to have what was rightfully his. Those who fall away choose to turn from the truth, but many times they return once they become tired of a sinful lifestyle. The result is already foreseen by God and the great joy of the father once the son returned reflects Gods joy when his children return.

Though many may have fallen, many have also received salvation. Pray for the return of the prodigals and the commencement of the great end-time revival to sweep the earth. *Today is the day of salvation (2 Corinthians 6:2).*

Knowledge will increase

Daniel 12:4 *But you, Daniel, roll up and seal the words of the scroll until the time of the end. Many will go here and there, and knowledge will increase.*

There is no doubt the age of the internet has ushered in an explosion of knowledge, such as never seen in history. Knowledge was once gained through books, experience, or revelation from God, but now we just need to click a button. Instead of asking God people are asking Google and algorithms take us to a seemingly endless stream of information. The access to information is scary and fascinating at the same time because the capabilities of self-learned geniuses or evil master minds can be hidden by anonymous IP addresses. The *dark Web* is a dangerous place where much evil exists.

Before the 1900s global knowledge increased approximately every century; by the end of World War 2 it was doubling every 25 years, today knowledge is doubling on average every 13 months, but soon, with the 5G roll out, global knowledge is expected to double every 12 hours! (38).

The human mind cannot decipher such information at such a high rate, it will turn the mind into scrambled eggs as information cannot be processed. Along with this increase in knowledge, microchips have been created that can be placed in your hand or head (sounds eerily familiar to Revelation 13:16-17). These chips can process data, unlock doors, and be used for buying or selling! 20 years ago, such a creation was just science fiction, now in places like Sweden this is a reality for many citizens, and some people love it! They even used this technology for Covid passports! (39). Technology has become the universal God of this age, praised for its algorithmic ingenuity, and worshipped by multitudes; technology is the forerunner of the coming mark of the beast and the beast system. Without a powerful global internet grid such as 5G or 6G the beast system would not successfully operate, and the masses cannot be fully controlled for the enforcement of the mark.

More on technology

How will the beast system operate? The technology to run the system has already been developed and is being used in certain countries to a degree. Chinas social credit score system and facial recognition network is already monitoring a majority of its 1.4 billion citizens. If citizens being monitored do not behave in accordance with communist regulations, then they have points deducted on their credit score and this will affect the way they live. China has also released a new digital currency called the digital Yuan, like Bitcoin but owned by the Communist party (40). Sweden is micro chipping citizens who volunteer to be chipped. Bill Gates has created a patent for a new currency with the following patent number that just happens to have the numbers 666 #WO2020060606 (41). Bill Gates has also invested one billion dollars to cover the world in surveillance satellites (www.telegraph.co.uk). Bill Gates is also buying acres of farmland (42) and invests heavily into vaccine companies (43), this Microsoft inventor has his finger in many pies. Covid has rapidly shifted the world more into digitalization and centralization of powers through banking and government. Using Covid as a scapegoat, globalists have been able to play the Covid card to usher in more digital control, and they have been able to do this with the people's compliance in the name of health and safety. All the pieces of this technocratic puzzle are beginning to fit together, the only thing missing is the arrival of the mastermind.

Sidenote about how China uses technology and information on its citizens. China can easily track citizens, and this especially applies to Christians who worship the true living God. The communist party holds president Xi as their God, and any who are found that will not revere him are ostracized from society or put into re-education camps. In these camps some endure hardship and possible torture, so that they can learn the ways of the communist party (44). However, once a mind has been renewed by God through His word and one faithfully walks in the ways of Jesus Christ, it is impossible for them to be re-educated. This example in China is a snippet of the control the antichrist will have, so much control that any who refuse the mark will be killed.

What about 5G?

5G has been secretly and openly rolling out globally for a few years. When the roll out first started many were skeptical and in some places, protests were held, but now this control grid is silently being set up without much resistance. The frequency used for 5G is the same frequency used by the military for dispersing crowds. The following information is a snippet taken from www.rfsafe.com/5g-network

Today's cellular and Wi-Fi networks rely on microwaves – a type of electromagnetic radiation utilizing frequencies up to 6 gigahertz (GHz) to wirelessly transmit voice and data. This era of wireless frequency is almost over, making room for new 5G applications that will require using new spectrum bands in much higher frequency ranges above 6 GHz to 100 GHz and beyond, utilizing submillimeter and millimeter waves.

Millimeter waves are utilized by the U.S Army in crowd dispersal guns called Active Denial Systems. Dr. Paul Ben-Ishai pointed to research that was commissioned by the U.S Army to find out why people ran away when the beam touched them. "If you are unlucky enough to be standing

there when it hits you, you will feel like your body is on fire". The U.S. Department of Defense explains how. "The sensation dissipates when the target moves out of the beam. The sensation is intense enough to cause a nearly instantaneous reflex action of the target to flee the beam".

Imagine the intensity of this frequency on a global scale when connected to the surveillance satellites invested by Mr. Gates. Some may argue that the waves used are less intense than military use, but when all these network systems are connected is the frequency less intense? Sure, faster internet is a handy tool, but if harm is being caused to humans is it worth the risk on such a scale without knowing long term effects?

This system of surveillance and control has been the plan of the elites for a long time. Who are the *elites?* A few names could be the following: *the Rockefellers, Rothschilds, Bilderberg* and secret societies that are not so secret anymore such as the *freemasons* and the *illuminati.* These renowned *elites* have a global takeover plan that's been handed down through generations. Discussing these groups in detail will require many books, but here is a snippet of the illuminati...

The illuminati were founded on the 1st of May 1776 by Adam Weishaupt. The vison of this group is *global domination by controlling them without dominating them* – (info Wikipedia – illuminati). How can a person or group control the masses without dominating them? You do it secretly through means such as predictive programming via films, television (tell-a-vision) and music; Chem-trails caused by contaminating the food we eat through chemicals, social media (Facebook, YouTube, Twitter), internet in some circumstances and even manipulating the weather through HARRP. Many will say these groups and such social conditioning is all conspiracy, no evidence backs up this information. Then Covid arrived, and the conspiracy theories of a *new world order* suddenly became more accepted. Most people have heard about the economic forums *great reset* initiative, the *fourth industrial revolution* to quote the words of the founder Klaus Schwab. Suddenly all these far-fetched *conspiracy theories* are not so hard to believe anymore. In 2030, *you will own nothing and be happy* - a quote from the economic forum. Why will you own nothing? Because the rich plan to own everything.

 Who is the real enemy? There is a demonic agenda disguised as a humanitarian plan. The agenda is called *Agenda 2021/Agenda 2030* – or we could call it the *New World Order/Great Reset.* Some of the ambitions considered are noble and praiseworthy, such as ending global poverty and protecting the planet. On the surface the agenda seems harmless, but many do not realize what needs to be done to achieve such an ambition, and how many people will not survive the transition phase due to extreme changes. For example, getting rid of gas or certain fossil fuels sounds good, but without a sufficient replacement this will lead to power outages, supply issues and food shortages, this has already started happening globally since 2020! Some blame Covid, lockdowns, war, mass spending by governments and the disruption of supply chains for the food crisis – but behind all this there is an agenda advancing. Why are all the areas most effected to do with gas, petrol, and food? Why have may food manufacturing factories been burned? Why have many food industries been hacked? (45 & 46) Is all this just a coincidence or is there a *Great Reset* being planned and for this reset to happen the old system must be systematically destroyed. Governments know that mass spending does not solve problems in the long term because it devalues the Fiat currency, this eventually leads to a financial collapse. Inflation is just the tip of the iceberg of the devastating consequences – all these things effect the common person! It can be blamed on this or that but ultimately looking deeper into the issue it is an obvious agenda being enforced and Covid/war are being used as the scapegoat.

Governments who have joined the United Nations may not realize the full extent of the plan; they are just playing their part. Behind the United Nations are the deep state governments/elite groups who are rarely heard of on mainstream platforms, behind the deep state are demonic influences. The enemies of this world are not humans but Spiritual entities that joined Satan in His rebellion against God. If Satan is the *God of this age,* then it should be no surprise that he is the mastermind behind globalization. God created nations and gave them their sovereignty; globalization is not of the God of Christianity! God said to Abraham, *"the nations will be blessed through you" (Genesis 22:18).* Getting rid of borders and national sovereignty is not Gods intended purpose. Despite all this, no doubt God can still work through governments for his purposes, for the *government rests upon his shoulders (Isaiah 9:6-7).* However, there is a dark agenda concealed in array of light and presented in a neat package for saving the world. If God had no intentions for nations, then Israel would have been forgotten.

Satan's agenda is to steer the world away from the one true God and have them worship something or someone else and eventually Satan himself through the antichrist. Many may claim not to believe in God and yet worship things/people like God such as money, sports, celebrities, the world itself, loved ones and any other things/persons that are highly exalted. If the enemy succeeds at turning people from God, it is much easier to manipulate and control them. As the saying goes, *those who stand for nothing fall for anything.* Gods people must stand for the truth revealed through His word, otherwise they may be deceived into believing the devils lies. This is the reason agenda 2030 is so dangerous! For this agenda to be fulfilled those leading the way must take absolute control over the lives of every citizen. Citizens do not like to be controlled so there will be a reaction, which then creates more control through severe methods such as martial law.

Satan wants to be worshipped as God, so ultimately all these agendas combined will lead to the worship of one man inhabited by Satan revealed at the time of the tribulation. The great convergence of end time signs is happening now – we are the blessed generation to see it all take place!

Believers in Christ are protected through faith. Jesus has given us *authority to tread on snakes and scorpions and all the power of the enemy without being harmed (Luke 10:19). You will walk through the fire, and it will not burn you (Isaiah 43:2).* Deadly frequencies, poison in the food supply, predictive programming, and extreme pressure to conform to the *new normal* need not steer the believer away from Christ, this should encourage the believer to trust God more – for all these things were written about! God has given His people power over the schemes of the enemy, even the secret unseen schemes. *For no weapon formed against you shall prosper (Isaiah 54:17).* The things coming upon the world should not cause us to fear but to pray and to seek God and His Kingdom. The time is now to reach the lost for salvation by sharing the love of Jesus with them. What is written must take place, if we cannot stop it then we can at least spread the gospel and snatch many from the flames of hell. While globalists seek to build a new world here on earth *Jesus is preparing a place for His people* (John 14:1-7). When the time is right, he will bring us into our eternal dwelling into a future so wonderful that human words cannot express it. The globalist will fail just as they failed when building the tower of Bebel, history does indeed repeat itself. Trust in the one who does not fail, who *holds the waters in his hands (Isaiah 40:12) who knows us even before we are born and predestined us for glory (Jeremiah*

1:5). Yes, trust in Him and reverently fear him. Satan has already lost the war; it was written and has been fulfilled!

Conclusion of the prophecies and signs of Christs return

Conclusion of prophecies.

Floods and wildfires could also be mentioned. Wildfires have destroyed much of the world's forests due to rises in global temperatures and arson attacks. The Amazon has lost much land to wildfires, and this is concerning due to the Amazon providing 20% of the world's oxygen. The culmination of these signs and the intensity is another sign of the soon arrival of Kind Jesus.

Top news stories do not linger for long periods unless there is a narrative being told. One day the news may show floods and wildfires and the next day the news is filled with Trumps presidency, Brexit, Covid or war. Yet behind the scenes of the main stage drama, floods, tornados, earthquakes, fires, volcanic eruptions, and many other disasters are taking place. Some may blame global warming; others may say Gods judgment has come – but do the righteous get judged with the unrighteous? The earth has had her fill of blood and *nature is groaning for restoration (Romans 8:22-23).* Just as labor pains increase before the child is born, so will all these things increase until Jesus returns.

Everything happening now is preparing the stage for the arrival of the antichrist who will appear to have all the answers to the questions people have.

Jesus said in Matthew 24 *"So, when you see standing in the holy place 'the abomination that causes desolation, 'spoken of through the prophet Daniel—let the reader understand— then let those who are in Judea flee to the mountains. Let no one on the housetop go down to take anything out of the house. Let no one in the field go back to get their cloak. How dreadful it will be in those days for pregnant women and nursing mothers! Pray that your flight will not take place in winter or on the Sabbath.*

For then there will be great distress, unequalled from the beginning of the world until now—and never to be equaled again. "If those days had not been cut short, no one would survive, but for the sake of the elect those days will be shortened. At that time if anyone says to you, 'Look, here is the Messiah!' or, 'There he is!' do not believe it. For false messiahs and false prophets will appear and perform great signs and wonders to deceive, if possible, even the elect.

There is a time coming soon when the antichrist will be revealed and will rule the world. Everything done by this man of sin, who will be the devil incarnate, will be opposite to Jesus Christ and the ways of God almighty. The world will be in such peril that Jesus refers to this as a time like no other in history – consider history, how bad this time must be!

There is hope during the tribulation. After these seven dark years Christ will rule for a thousand years! The darkness of those days will be extinguished by the splendor of the Lords second coming, when the true light will take his place and rule the earth. Satanists refer to Lucifer as the light bearer and Jesus as the enemy, their Kingdom is upside down and is doomed for destruction. During the thousand-year reign earth will experience true and lasting peace, such as has never been seen since the fall of humanity. The devil will be *bound in the bottomless pit so he cannot deceive the nations anymore* (Revelation 20:3). Sin will still be in people's hearts, but Christ will settle disputes during this time and earth will be populated like never before! *The wolf also shall dwell with the lamb, and the leopard lie down with the kid; and the calf and the young lion and the fatling together; and a little child shall lead them (Isaiah 11:6),* even the animal Kingdom will be at peace! This is truly a time to desire to be a part of.

The signs of Christs return

There is no need for someone to tell you Jesus has returned, if they do, they are lying. The second coming of Christ will be so spectacular that *even those who pierced him will see him. Look, he is coming with the clouds, and every eye will see him, even those who pierced him – Revelation 1:7.* The second coming of Christ will not be told, it will be displayed...

Matthew 24:29-31 *"Immediately after the distress of those days, the sun will be darkened, and the moon will not give its light; the stars will fall from the sky, and the heavenly bodies will be shaken". Then will appear the sign of the son of man in heaven. And then all the peoples of the earth will mourn when they see the son of man coming on the clouds of heaven, with power and great glory. And he will send his angels with a loud trumpet call, and they will gather his elect from the four winds, from one end of the heavens to the other.*

What a powerful entrance this will be! Two distinctions can be considered concerning Christs return. First, He does not return before the distress of the tribulation, but immediately after this time. The word *immediately* is a reminder of when the apostle Peter started to sink when walking on water and Jesus *immediately* grabbed him (Matthew 14:31). It is an immediate snatching of Gods elect as Jesus returns to the earth. Second, the elect of God (those chosen before the foundation of the world – Ephesians 1:4), are not gathered to Christ until after the distress of those days. Whether this includes every believer or only those at the time of the tribulation is not specified in this verse, nevertheless, there will be a great harvest at this time.

The time of Christs return is at hand due to the fulfillment of many prophecies, all though *nobody knows the time or hour of His return except the father (Matthew 24:36, Matthew 25:13)* we can certainly know the season.

*Matthew 24:32-34 Now learn a lesson from the fig tree: As soon as its twigs get tender and its leaves come out, you know that summer is near. Even so, **when you see all these things**, you know that it is near, right at the door. Truly I tell you, this generation will not pass away until all these things have happened. Heaven and earth will pass away, but my words will never pass away.*

The earth is almost ripe for the return of Jesus. During this time of chaos, some will still be getting on with life by eating, drinking, and marrying – just as it was in Noah's day before he entered the ark (Matthew 24:38). Jesus *will come like a thief in the night* (1 Thessalonians 5:2), all though we may know the season, the time is still unknown; so, it is best to always be ready.

What about the rapture?

The word rapture, which derives from the Latin word rapio and Greek word harpazo means: *Caught up.* The verses used in relation to the rapture are found in the following...

1 Thessalonians 4:17 *Then we who are alive, who are left, will be **caught up** together with them in the clouds to meet the Lord in the air, and so we will always be with the Lord. Therefore encourage one another with these words.* Emphasis added

1 Corinthians 15:52 *In a moment, in the twinkling of an eye, at the last trumpet. For the trumpet will sound, and the dead will be raised imperishable, and we shall be changed.*

Luke 21:34-36 *But watch yourselves lest your hearts be weighed down with dissipation and drunkenness and cares of this life, and that day come upon you suddenly like a trap. For it will come upon all who dwell on the face of the earth. But always stay awake, praying that you may have strength to escape all these things that are going to take place, and to stand before the son of man.*

These verses are the clearest examples of what could be the rapture event. Many Christians are unsure on whether there is a rapture, or when the rapture will take place if there is such an event. There have been 4 modern day theories circulating on when the rapture is going to happen for those who believe in it.
1) pre-tribulation
2) mid-tribulation
3) post-tribulation.
4) pre-wrath rapture

In the basic form this means...
A rapture before the tribulation begins, which means the rapture is imminent and could be at any moment.
A rapture in the middle of the tribulation when we have reached 3 and a half years.
A rapture at the end of the 7-year tribulation.
A rapture before God pours out his wrath on the earth.

Christians have not been able to say with 100% certainty when it will be (though some have made the claim), but many refer to the pre-tribulation as the one that makes more sense as this is the only imminent option. The other option that also makes complete sense is the pre-wrath rapture, this is because the children of God have not been appointed to wrath.

None of this information is to credit or discredit the belief of the rapture; but instead has been written for information purposes and for a deeper understanding of the importance of our faith in Christ.

The bible is clear on two things:

First, there are some of Gods people that endure the tribulation as we can see in Revelation 14:12 *this calls for patient endurance on the part of the people of God who keep his commands and remain faithful to Jesus.* It is clear in revelation that "some" of Gods people are certainly around during the tribulation. The question is whether "Gods people" refers to the church, the Jews or those termed as *tribulation saints,* but this is something that is relevant for a much deeper study. Second, clearly a certain group of believers will not taste death, they will be like Elijah or Enoch, who were caught up to God without dying, we can see this clearly because Jesus said in Luke 21:36 *But always stay awake, praying that you may have strength to escape all these things that are going to take place, and to stand before the son of man.* Also, in 1 Thessalonians 4:17 it says that *we who are alive and left will be caught up in the air with the Lord.*

Some believers have turned the rapture into a comfort blanket to escape the antichrists persecution. The *escape all these things* or *the hour of testing (Revelation 3:10)* does not specifically relate to persecution but is more likely when Gods wrath is poured out onto humanity. The *blessed hope* as the rapture is termed, is not only for a specific time when believers are caught up, but also for every day of the believer's earthly life, because any day could be the last. Christians will face persecution (Matthew 10:16-25) and tribulations (John 16:33) during this life, it could be argued that the tribulations referred to by Jesus does not include the great tribulation, but this is not specified in the bible. History also proves Christians have suffered much persecution. However, Christians are certainly not appointed to Gods wrath, the question then is, how much of the tribulation is Gods wrath, and how much of it is Satan's? The word says, *wo to the inhabitants of the earth, for Satan has come down with great wrath, for he hath but a short time (Revelation 12:12).* The tribulation

74

includes both Gods and Satan's wrath. Noah was protected from the wrath of God, but he faced much tribulation (Genesis chapters 5-10).

For God has not appointed the believer to wrath but to obtain salvation by our Lord Jesus Christ (1 Thessalonians 5:9).

Believers cannot depend on being raptured the moment persecution comes, if they do and do not get caught up, how can they keep their hope? However, if they rest in the promise that Christ is with us always, *even to the end of age (Matthew 28:20)* then they will have strength to endure. When Gods wrath is poured out, He can and will protect his children, whether this means removing them from the earth or protecting them while still on earth, like He did with Noah and family. Whether we face the tribulation or not, our blessed eternal hope is in Jesus Christ – if He is our hope then we will never be disappointed.

Believers should live with a constant readiness to meet the Lord; Jesus can come for us personally at any moment. Falling out with fellow believers because we differ on the timing of the rapture is not a good testimony to the world. *By the love we have for each other we are known as Christs disciples (John 13:35).* It is better to teach people readiness and how to be a faithful witness for Jesus without referring to the rapture. Live like the five faithful virgins that filled up their lamps with oil (Matthew 25), instead of like the five who did not prepare to meet the Lord. Living this way means we will never be caught by surprise when the Lord returns.

Is the church the one holding back the antichrist? *When He who restrains is taken out of the way, then the antichrist will be revealed* (2 Thessalonians 2:7). Yet the bible does not state who *he* is all though some speculations have been provided concerning this such as the *church, government,* the *right hand of God* or even

Satan himself. All these speculations could be justified, let's look at them...

The church... If the tribulation is the time of *Jacobs trouble* (Jeremiah 30:7, Daniel 12:1-4), then how can this involve the church? Jacob refers to the Jews, therefore some would argue that the tribulation is about the salvation of the Jews and judgement for the world. Also, the church is not mentioned after chapter 6 of the book of revelation, therefore they are not present during this time. The term commonly used for Gods people during this time is saints. This is a very logical viewpoint for pre-tribulation rapture. However, the church does not restrain evil, if it did then many places such as North Korea or China would not have such totalitarian regimes. Just as Jesus did not hold back evil when arrested and nailed to a cross – evil is permitted sometimes by the will of God and even the light of God Himself did not restrain it. *For if people do these things when the tree is green, what will they do when it is dry (Luke 23:31).* Also, many types of antichrists have risen over the last 2 millennial, the church did not prevent them from rising.

Government... Government was instituted to usher in law and order. *When the righteous thrive, the people rejoice; when the wicked rule, the people groan* (Proverbs 29:2). Since America has been the world superpower Western civilization has flourished like no other time in history. Democracy paved a way for entrepreneurs, innovations, and transformation to society. Un-corrupted governments have the power to make decisions that create a better society – not a perfect one, just a better one. When good men and women lead and hold positions of great influence, they can keep back evil to a certain extent. However, evil still prevails in some cases as during the rule of America there has been many wars, including World War 1 & 2.

The right hand of God... The right hand of God is shown throughout scripture as a symbol of strength; removed to allow the enemies attack or stretched out to bring judgement against them (Lamentations 2:3,4, Isaiah 62:8, Psalm 21:8, Psalm 60:5, Psalm 138:7...). If Gods right hand held back the enemy in the Old Testament wars, why could He not do the same with the antichrist? The tribulation is a time that has been sealed by God, only to be revealed at the end for Daniels 70th week (Daniel 9:24-27). It makes sense that God would be restraining the last antichrist until the final time. However, this is not stated and therefore is also just a theory.

Satan himself... Many believe that Satan longs for this time for the antichrist to rule, but why would He? When Satan is cast out of heaven, he comes down to earth with great fury, because he *hath but a short time*. The devil knows time is short the moment the antichrist steps on the scene, so perhaps He would be aiming to keep the antichrist back for as long as possible. As plausible as this view seems, it does not make much sense. For example, the tribulation is a time set apart from God, not the devil, therefore the devil is not the one to determine when it begins. God is the one who deals with the sins of the world, Israel and perhaps the church during this period – should the true church of Christ remain. God is in control of all of it despite this being the worst time in human history.

   If the church is the one holding back the antichrist, we will soon be finding out. 1 Peter 5:8 *Be sober, be vigilant; because you adversary the devil, as a walking lion, walks about, seeking whom he may devour.* Be equipped with the full armor of God. Ephesians 6:15-17 *Stand firm then, with the belt of truth buckled around your waist, with the breastplate of righteousness in place, and with your feet fitted with the readiness that comes from the gospel of peace. In addition to all this, take up the shield of faith, with which you can extinguish all the flaming arrows of the evil one. Take the helmet of salvation and the sword of the Spirit, which is the word of God.* If we do this, we will stand when the day of evil comes.

All the believer in Christ needs to do is draw near to Jesus daily and trust that he will guide us through everything we must face by his spirit's power. We are commanded to *not be afraid* (Isaiah 41:10) to *trust with all our hearts* (Proverbs 3:5) and *rejoice in the joy of our salvation* (Psalm 51:12) If we do this, then the Devil can never defeat us, and we will persevere. We can see through the lens of the bible that everything Jesus spoke about in Matthew 24 is already taking place with great acceleration. Other prophecies are yet to be fulfilled such as the building of the third temple (Daniel 9:24-27) or the war of Psalm 83, nevertheless, there is no denying that the end is right at the door. **May the believer look up because their redemption draws near** (Luke 21:28)

Eternal hope

If you made it this far in the book and do not know Jesus Christ as Lord and savior, you are not without hope! The world cannot offer you eternal security, but only temporary hope that depends on external peace. Let's be real, external peace on earth has never been long lasting, evil people always find a way to destroy the peace. However, internal peace cannot be stolen, and eternal hope found through Christ cannot be shaken. You may have had a bad experience with a church or Christian that did not reflect who Christ is, for this reason you wanted nothing to do with God. If you were not shown love and offered the opportunity to be forgiven by God, then you were not shown who God is! Every person on earth falls short of Gods perfect standards, but that's okay, because Christ was given to exchange our imperfect record with his perfect one! The beautiful exchange happens when you believe and put your trust in Christ. We cannot earn salvation, it is a gift of God, *for it is by grace that we are saved* (Ephesians 2:8-9). So, if you want to know who the real God is then turn to Jesus today. You are never too messed up to come to Jesus, if you were, then Christ would not have died on the cross for you.

References

1) Donald Trump's Stance on Illegal Immigration (managementstudyguide.com)
2) Trump Didn't Bribe Ukraine. It's Actually Worse Than That. - POLITICO Magazine
3) Why Trump Moving US Embassy to Jerusalem Infuriates the Middle East (businessinsider.com)
4) Amid COVID-19 pandemic, empty store shelves are showing people's concerns - Medill Reports Chicago (northwestern.edu)
5) President Zelensky refuses to leave Ukraine, asks for ammunition instead of 'a ride' | Marca
6) Australia's COVID concentration camps: A quick rundown – Thuletide (wordpress.com)
7) Israel Makes COVID Booster Shot Mandatory - The Media Line
8) WATCH: Biden says 'there's going to be a new world order' and US must take lead | Washington Examiner
9) World Economic Forum and the New World Order – Rights and Freedoms (wordpress.com)
10) china's 70th anniversary military parade - Search (bing.com)
11) North Korea: Footage of military celebrations for 70th anniversary - BBC News
12) Will Trump's Middle East Peace Plan Work? (newsweekpakistan.com)
13) Ahmadinejad: Wipe Israel off map | News | Al Jazeera
14) Israeli threat to attack Iran over nuclear weapons | Israel | The Guardian
15) United States recognition of Jerusalem as capital of Israel - Wikipedia
16) Iran and Russia: A Partnership in the Making | Middle East Institute (mei.edu)
17) US China Trade War: Timelines, Statistics, Maps, and More - Fortunly

18) China threatens to invade Taiwan with fears of all-out War - London Business News | Londonlovesbusiness.com
19) Anton LaVey - Wikipedia
20) Mormonism - Wikipedia
21) Background: Life Before the Holocaust (bl.uk)
22) anti-Semitism | History, Facts, & Examples | Britannica
23) Crusades: Definition, Religious Wars & Facts - HISTORY
24) Catholic Church sexual abuse cases by country - Wikipedia
25) The Major Religions In India - WorldAtlas
26) Dead Sea Scrolls discoveries are first ancient Bible texts to be found in 60 years (nbcnews.com)
27) Japan earthquake and tsunami of 2011 | Facts & Death Toll | Britannica
28) Britain's knife epidemic laid bare as cops face 30 blade crimed a DAY across the country (the-sun.com)
29) Every mass shooting in the US – a visual database | US news | The Guardian
30) Jesus didn't turn anyone away... (shanktified.com)
31) Sex reassignment surgery (male-to-female) - Wikipedia
32) Man, 19, Regrets 'Frankenstein Hack Job' Gender Reassignment Surgery (dailysignal.com)
33) What is China's Social Credit System and What Does it Mean for Online Identity? - SelfKey
34) Persecution of Christians - Wikipedia
35) 'Don't pray for the persecution to stop,' says Middle East Christian woman | Christian Times
36) Well-known Christian author, purity advocate, renounces his faith: 'I hope you can forgive me' | Fox News
37) I haven't 'renounced' my faith but it's on 'incredibly shaky ground', says Marty Sampson (christiantoday.com)
38) www.industrytap.com/knowledgedoublingeverytwelvehours

39) Sweden Starts Microchipping COVID Passports in People | Newsmax.com

40) China's digital yuan: What is it and how does it work? (cnbc.com)

41) Bill Gates Crytocurrency Patent Edging Us Closer to Dystopian Society and Mark of the Beast – Coercion Code – "Dark Times are upon us"

42) Bill Gates reveals reasons behind massive farmland purchases: Developing genetically modified crops to develop biofuels (climatesciencenews.com)

43) Bill Gates and the Return on Investment in Vaccinations (cnbc.com)

44) Xinjiang internment camps - Wikipedia

45) A List Of 16 Major Fires That Have Occurred At Key Food Industry Facilities In US Since Start Of 2022 - The Washington Standard

46) Cyberattack on food supply followed years of warnings - POLITICO